ISBN 0-8373-2012-7

C-2012   CAREER EXAMINATION SERIES

This is your
PASSBOOK® for...

Game Warden

Test Preparation Study Guide

Questions & Answers

NATIONAL LEARNING CORPORATION

PASSBOOK®

NOTICE

PASSBOOK SERIES®

THE *PASSBOOK SERIES®* has been created to prepare applicants and candidates for the ultimate academic battlefield – the examination room.

At some time in our lives, each and every one of us may be required to take an examination – for validation, matriculation, admission, qualification, registration, certification, or licensure.

Based on the assumption that every applicant or candidate has met the basic formal educational standards, has taken the required number of courses, and read the necessary texts, the *PASSBOOK SERIES®* furnishes the one special preparation which may assure passing with confidence, instead of failing with insecurity. Examination questions – together with answers – are furnished as the basic vehicle for study so that the mysteries of the examination and its compounding difficulties may be eliminated or diminished by a sure method.

This book is meant to help you pass your examination provided that you qualify and are serious in your objective.

The entire field is reviewed through the huge store of content information which is succinctly presented through a provocative and challenging approach – the question-and-answer method.

A climate of success is established by furnishing the correct answers at the end of each test.

You soon learn to recognize types of questions, forms of questions, and patterns of questioning. You may even begin to anticipate expected outcomes.

You perceive that many questions are repeated or adapted so that you can gain acute insights, which may enable you to score many sure points.

You learn how to confront new questions, or types of questions, and to attack them confidently and work out the correct answers.

You note objectives and emphases, and recognize pitfalls and dangers, so that you may make positive educational adjustments.

Moreover, you are kept fully informed in relation to new concepts, methods, practices, and directions in the field.

You discover that you are actually taking the examination all the time: you are preparing for the examination by "taking" an examination, not by reading extraneous and/or supererogatory textbooks.

In short, this PASSBOOK®, used directedly, should be an important factor in helping you to pass your test.

U.S. Fish and Wildlife Service

The United States Fish and Wildlife Service is the principal agency through which the Federal Government carries out its responsibilities for managing the Nation's wild birds, mammals, and fish for the enjoyment of all people.

The Service's national responsibilities for fish and wildlife go back over 100 years to the establishment in 1871 of a predecessor agency, the Bureau of Fisheries. First created as an independent agency, the Bureau of Fisheries was later placed in the Department of Commerce. A second predecessor agency, the Bureau of Biological Survey, was established in 1885 in the Department of Agriculture.

The two Bureaus and their functions were transferred in 1939 to the Department of the Interior. They were consolidated into one agency and redesignated the Fish and Wildlife Service in 1940. Further reorganization came in 1956 when the Fish and Wildlife Act created the United States Fish and Wildlife Service and provided for it to replace and succeed the former Fish and Wildlife Service. The Act established two Bureaus within the new Service: the Bureau of Commercial Fisheries and the Bureau of Sport Fisheries and Wildlife.

In 1970, the Bureau of Commercial Fisheries was transferred to the Department of Commerce. The Bureau of Sport Fisheries and Wildlife remained in Interior and was designated by Act of Congress in April 1974 as the United States Fish and Wildlife Service.

Today the Service consists of a headquarters office in Washington, D.C., six regional offices, an Alaska area office, and over 700 field units and installations. These include more than 375 national wildlife refuges comprising more than 33 million acres; 35 fish and wildlife research stations and laboratories; 45 cooperative research units at universities across the country; nearly 100 national fish hatcheries; and a nationwide network of wildlife law enforcement agents and wildlife biologists.

Program activities include:

—Biological monitoring through scientific research; surveillance of pesticides, heavy metals and thermal pollution; studies of fish and wildlife populations; ecological studies.

—Environmental impact assessment through river basin studies, including hydroelectric dams, nuclear powersites, stream channelization, and dredge and fill permits; associated research; environmental impact statement review.

—Area planning and preservation involving river basin and wilderness areas; special studies such as oil shale and geothermal energy.

—Migratory birds; wildlife refuge management for production, migration, and wintering; game law enforcement; bird banding, harvest and survival rate studies; breeding, migrating, and wintering surveys; disease studies.

—Mammals and nonmigratory birds; wildlife refuge management of resident species (primarily big game); law enforcement; research on disease and population distribution, including marine mammals and species transplants; technical assistance.

—Animal damage control; operational measures through cooperative programs

to control predator, rodent, and bird depredations on crops and livestock; research on nonlethal control methods and predator-prey relationships.

—Cooperative fish and wildlife research units located at universities to conduct research and supervise graduate student research, complementing the Service's wildlife and fishery research programs.

—Coastal anadromous fish; hatchery production; research on nutrition, disease, and habitat requirements in 16 of the 24 coastal States.

—Great Lakes fisheries; hatchery production of lake trout; fishery management in cooperation with

Canada and the States; research; sea lamprey control.

—Inland and reservoir fisheries; hatchery production; management of Federal, military and Indian waters; control of fish diseases and undesirable fish; technical assistance; training; research on fish diseases; genetics, nutrition, taxonomy and cultural methods.

—Providing national and international leadership in the area of endangered fish, wildlife, and plants from the standpoint of both restorations as well as preventive measures involving threatened species. This program includes development of species lists; research on propagation methods; distribution, genetics, and behavior; operation of wildlife refuges; law enforcement; foreign importation and exportation enforcement; consultant services to foreign countries; consultant services to other Federal agencies and cooperative management with the States.

—Youth programs to further the development of the natural resources of the United States and to provide meaningful employment for young men and women. This program is operated in joint participation with the U.S. Department of Labor.

CAREERS
in the U.S. Fish and Wildlife Service

The interrelationships of fish and wildlife with water, land, industry, and people are very complex. Occupations in the Service require specialized education and/or experience. While an interest in conservation is desirable, academic training in fish and wildlife biology is essential for most positions.

Service managers make every effort to place employees in positions for which they are best qualified and in which they will have a chance to develop to their full potential. Most competitive appointments in the Service are to such positions as wildlife biologist, fishery biologist, refuge manager, special agent, technical aid, as well as administrative, clerical, secretarial, and other support positions.

Because of the wide variety of diversified fish and wildlife programs administered by the Service in all States and the trust territories, career and executive development concepts highlight job mobility. Accordingly, professional employees appointed in the Service must be mobile and available for transfer to various locations throughout their career.

Wildlife Biologist

Wildlife biologists study the distribution, abundance, habits, life histories, ecology, mortality factors, and economic values of birds, mammals, and other wildlife. They plan or carry out wildlife management programs, determine conditions and problems affecting wildlife, apply research findings to the management of wildlife, restore or develop wildlife habitats, regulate wildlife populations, and control wildlife diseases.

Fishery Biologist

Fishery biologists study the life history, habits, classification, and economic relations of aquatic organisms. They manage fish hatcheries and fishery resources and gather data on interrelations between species of fish and the effects of natural and human changes in the environment on the survival and growth of fish. Fishery biologists determine rearing and stocking methods best adapted for maximum success in fish hatchery operations and devise methods to regulate fishing to secure an optimum sustained yield.

Research Positions

Wildlife biologists, fishery biologist, ecologists, and other related specialists at research facilities conduct detailed research in environmental contaminate evaluation, migratory bird and marine mammal studies, population ecology and habitat evaluation and assessment, fish husbandry including nutrition and genetics, and related studies concerning fish and wildlife populations.

Refuge Manager

Refuge managers manage national wildlife refuges to protect and preserve migratory and native species of birds, mammals, endangered species, and other forms of wildlife. They are responsible for providing a balanced wildlife management program at the refuge as well as public use programs.

Special Agent (Wildlife) and Special Agent (Wildlife)(Pilot)

Special agents investigate violations of Federal laws within the enforcement jurisdiction of the Department of the Interior for the protection and conservation of wildlife, including birds, mammals, fishes, reptiles, mollusks, and crustacea. Investigations involve surveillance, participation in raids, interviewing witnesses, interrogating suspects, searching for physical evidence and clues, seizing contraband, making arrests, and other enforcement activities. Special Agent (Wildlife)(Pilot), in addition to the above duties, pilot aircraft in connection with law enforcement activities. See page 10 for additional information.

Aid-Type Positions

Fish and wildlife aids and technicians provide support to professional biologists in a wide range of laboratory and field station operations such as laboratory analysis and testing, field surveys, and numerous paraprofessional activities.

District Field Assistant

District field assistants are employed in the Western States and are engaged in various duties associated with controlling damage by predatory animals and rodents.

Because this work is conducted in cooperation with States, counties, livestock associations, and others, district field assistant positions are not under the competitive Civil Service system. Inquiries concerning employment opportunities may be addressed to the Service offices listed on page 15.

Opportunities in Trades and Crafts

Maintenance workers, light and heavy equipment operators, laborers, and some skilled trade workers are employed at wildlife refuges, fish hatcheries, and research laboratories. Hiring is conducted through local offices of the Civil Service Commission from eligible candidates on appropriate Civil Service registers. Salaries are based on prevailing wages in the local hiring area.

General Qualification Requirements

The table below shows examples of basic qualifications for most professional positions:

GRADE   MINIMUM REQUIREMENTS

GS-5   Bachelor's degree in an appropriate field.

GS-7   Bachelor's degree with B or better average, or
Bachelor's degree plus 1 year of appropriate experience or 1 full year of graduate study.

GS-9   Bachelor's degree plus:
2 years appropriate experience, or
2 full years of graduate study, or
1 year of appropriate experience, and 1 full year of graduate study.

GS-11   Bachelor's degree plus:
3 years appropriate experience, or
2 years appropriate experience, and 1 full year of graduate study, or
1 year of appropriate experience, and
2 full years of graduate study, or Ph.D.

Summer Employment

Most summer positions are at field station locations. Positions at grades GS-1 through GS-4 are filled by eligibles from the Civil Service Commission Summer Employment Examination. The examination announcement may be obtained from local offices of the Civil Service Commission in the fall of each year.

Appointments in the Fish and Wildlife Service

Most positions in the Service are under the competitive Civil Service system; that is, positions are filled by candidates who are on U.S. Civil Service registers as a result of establishing eligibility through a competitive Civil Service examination. Initial appointment in a permanent position is followed by a probationary or trial period of one year. Appointments are made to positions in the U.S. Fish and Wildlife Service without regard to race, color, age, religion, politics, national origin, sex, or any other nonmerit factor.

Specific College Course Requirements

Wildlife Biologist:

30 semester hours, or equivalent, in biological sciences, including
9 semester hours in wildlife subjects
12 semester hours in zoology
9 semester hours in botany or related plant sciences

Fishery Biologist:

30 semester hours, or equivalent, in biological sciences, including
6 semester hours in aquatic subjects
12 semester hours in animal sciences

Refuge Manager:

9 semester hours, or equivalent, in zoology
6 semester hours in wildlife courses
9 semester hours in botany

Additional course work is required for wildlife and fishery research positions. Refer to the current Civil Service Commission examination announcement for these additional requirements.

Qualifications Requirements for Special Agents

Except for the substitutions provided below, candidates must have had experience of the length shown in the table and of the nature described in the paragraphs following:

Grade	General experience (years)	Specialized experience (years)	Total experience (years)
GS–5	3	0	3
GS–7	3	1	4
GS–9	3	2	5
GS–11 and above	3	3	6

General Experience

Progressively responsible experience which has demonstrated ability to work and deal effectively with individuals or groups of persons; skill in collecting and assembling pertinent facts; ability to prepare clear and concise reports; and, ability and willingness to accept responsibility. Professional level work in one of the biological sciences meets the general experience requirement.

Specialized Experience

Progressively responsible experience in criminal or comparable investigative activity which demonstrated initiative, ingenuity, resourcefulness, and judgment in collecting, assembling, and developing facts; ability to logically and objectively analyze and evaluate facts, evidence, and related information; skill in preparing written and oral reports and presenting investigative findings in a clear and concise manner; and, tact, discretion, and capability in obtaining cooperation and confidence of others. One year of professional experience in one of the biological sciences equivalent to at least grade GS–5 will meet the specialized experience requirement for grade GS–7.

NOTE: Experience as a U.S. Deputy Game Warden is not acceptable as qualifying for either general or specialized experience.

To qualify for a Special Agent (Wildlife) position at GS–11 and above, candidates must have previous experience in the investigation and enforcement of fish and wildlife laws.

Substitution of Education for Experience

General Experience

Study successfully completed in an accredited college or university may be substituted at the rate of 1 year of study (30 semester hours or equivalent) for 9 months of experience up to 4 years of study for 3 years of general experience. Therefore, a 4-year college degree, in any major, is fully qualifying at the GS–5 level.

Specialized Experience

One full year of graduate study in an accredited college or university in law enforcement, police administration, criminology, biological science, or in a criminal justice discipline may be substituted for the one year specialized experience requirement at the GS-7 level. Two full years of graduate work or the completion of the requirements for a master's degree in one of the above-mentioned majors may be substituted for the two-year specialized experience requirement at the GS-9 level. Completion of a total of at least 6 years of legal and prelegal education which meets all the requirements for an LL.B or J.D. degree will also provide eligibility, in full, at the GS-9 level.

Physical Requirements

Candidates for Special Agent (Wildlife) positions must meet the physical standards prescribed for this occupation and once employed, are included in a comprehensive physical examination program throughout their career. The medical standards for these positions are not waived for any candidate. Preemployment physical examination is at the candidate's expense. Copies of the medical standards are available upon request.

Investigation of Suitability

During the one-year probationary period, new employees undergo a full field background suitability investigation. A satisfactory full field investigation must be completed for all nonprobationary candidates prior to appointment.

Rating Procedures

Candidates at the GS-5 and GS-7 levels from outside the Federal service must pass a written test in addition to meeting the experience requirements. Procedures for applying to take the test are explained in CSC Announcement 432. The announcement is available at local CSC Federal Job Information Centers. Candidates at the GS-9 and above levels from outside the Federal service apply under the appropriate Mid- and Senior-Level Civil Service Examination in Washington, D.C. No written test is required.

All applicants must possess a valid automobile license at the time of appointment and retain such license throughout his/her tenure as a Special Agent (Wildlife).

Fish and Wildlife Management Training

Colleges and universities in many States offer courses in fish and wildlife

management or closely related fields. The schools of your choice can furnish information on courses and degrees offered.

Other Positions

Appointment to most positions, other than professional positions in the biological sciences, requires a written test as prescribed by the appropriate examination announcement.

We suggest that you contact the nearest Civil Service Commission office to obtain a copy of the examination announcement in which you are interested. Ask for the announcement by job or examination title.

The announcement will tell you what the jobs pay, where they are located, what the work is like, and what experience and training are required.

Workweek

The basic workweek consists of five eight-hour days, usually Monday through Friday. At some field stations it is necessary to adjust the working days to provide coverage seven days a week. This is essential to handle visitor use at a facility or to provide for the care and security of fish or confined wildlife, or a combination of both.

The Service has field operations of some type in every State. Listed on page 15 of this booklet are the addresses of the regional offices of the Service.

HOW TO TAKE A TEST

I. YOU MUST PASS AN EXAMINATION

A. *WHAT EVERY CANDIDATE SHOULD KNOW*

Examination applicants often ask us for help in preparing for the written test. What can I study in advance? What kinds of questions will be asked? How will the test be given? How will the papers be graded?

As an applicant for a civil service examination, you may be wondering about some of these things. Our purpose here is to suggest effective methods of advance study and to describe civil service examinations.

Your chances for success on this examination can be increased if you know how to prepare. Those "pre-examination jitters" can be reduced if you know what to expect. You can even experience an adventure in good citizenship if you know why civil service exams are given.

B. *WHY ARE CIVIL SERVICE EXAMINATIONS GIVEN?*

Civil service examinations are important to you in two ways. As a citizen, you want public jobs filled by employees who know how to do their work. As a job seeker, you want a fair chance to compete for that job on an equal footing with other candidates. The best-known means of accomplishing this two-fold goal is the competitive examination.

Exams are widely publicized throughout the nation. They may be administered for jobs in federal, state, city, municipal, town or village governments or agencies.

Any citizen may apply, with some limitations, such as the age or residence of applicants. Your experience and education may be reviewed to see whether you meet the requirements for the particular examination. When these requirements exist, they are reasonable and applied consistently to all applicants. Thus, a competitive examination may cause you some uneasiness now, but it is your privilege and safeguard.

C. *HOW ARE CIVIL SERVICE EXAMS DEVELOPED?*

Examinations are carefully written by trained technicians who are specialists in the field known as "psychological measurement," in consultation with recognized authorities in the field of work that the test will cover. These experts recommend the subject matter areas or skills to be tested; only those knowledges or skills important to your success on the job are included. The most reliable books and source materials available are used as references. Together, the experts and technicians judge the difficulty level of the questions.

Test technicians know how to phrase questions so that the problem is clearly stated. Their ethics do not permit "trick" or "catch" questions. Questions may have been tried out on sample groups, or subjected to statistical analysis, to determine their usefulness.

Written tests are often used in combination with performance tests, ratings of training and experience, and oral interviews. All of these measures combine to form the best-known means of finding the right person for the right job.

II. HOW TO PASS THE WRITTEN TEST

A. NATURE OF THE EXAMINATION

To prepare intelligently for civil service examinations, you should know how they differ from school examinations you have taken. In school you were assigned certain definite pages to read or subjects to cover. The examination questions were quite detailed and usually emphasized memory. Civil service exams, on the other hand, try to discover your present ability to perform the duties of a position, plus your potentiality to learn these duties. In other words, a civil service exam attempts to predict how successful you will be. Questions cover such a broad area that they cannot be as minute and detailed as school exam questions.

In the public service similar kinds of work, or positions, are grouped together in one "class." This process is known as *position-classification*. All the positions in a class are paid according to the salary range for that class. One class title covers all of these positions, and they are all tested by the same examination.

B. FOUR BASIC STEPS

1) Study the announcement

How, then, can you know what subjects to study? Our best answer is: "Learn as much as possible about the class of positions for which you've applied." The exam will test the knowledge, skills and abilities needed to do the work.

Your most valuable source of information about the position you want is the official exam announcement. This announcement lists the training and experience qualifications. Check these standards and apply only if you come reasonably close to meeting them.

The brief description of the position in the examination announcement offers some clues to the subjects which will be tested. Think about the job itself. Review the duties in your mind. Can you perform them, or are there some in which you are rusty? Fill in the blank spots in your preparation.

Many jurisdictions preview the written test in the exam announcement by including a section called "Knowledge and Abilities Required," "Scope of the Examination," or some similar heading. Here you will find out specifically what fields will be tested.

2) Review your own background

Once you learn in general what the position is all about, and what you need to know to do the work, ask yourself which subjects you already know fairly well and which need improvement. You may wonder whether to concentrate on improving your strong areas or on building some background in your fields of weakness. When the announcement has specified "some knowledge" or "considerable knowledge," or has used adjectives like "beginning principles of…" or "advanced … methods," you can get a clue as to the number and difficulty of questions to be asked in any given field. More questions, and hence broader coverage, would be included for those subjects which are more important in the work. Now weigh your strengths and weaknesses against the job requirements and prepare accordingly.

3) Determine the level of the position

Another way to tell how intensively you should prepare is to understand the level of the job for which you are applying. Is it the entering level? In other words, is this the position in which beginners in a field of work are hired? Or is it an intermediate or advanced level? Sometimes this is indicated by such words as "Junior" or "Senior" in the class title. Other jurisdictions use Roman numerals to designate the level – Clerk I, Clerk II, for example. The word "Supervisor" sometimes appears in the title. If the level is not indicated by the title, check the description of duties. Will you be working under very close supervision, or will you have responsibility for independent decisions in this work?

4) Choose appropriate study materials

Now that you know the subjects to be examined and the relative amount of each subject to be covered, you can choose suitable study materials. For beginning level jobs, or even advanced ones, if you have a pronounced weakness in some aspect of your training, read a modern, standard textbook in that field. Be sure it is up to date and has general coverage. Such books are normally available at your library, and the librarian will be glad to help you locate one. For entry-level positions, questions of appropriate difficulty are chosen – neither highly advanced questions, nor those too simple. Such questions require careful thought but not advanced training.

If the position for which you are applying is technical or advanced, you will read more advanced, specialized material. If you are already familiar with the basic principles of your field, elementary textbooks would waste your time. Concentrate on advanced textbooks and technical periodicals. Think through the concepts and review difficult problems in your field.

These are all general sources. You can get more ideas on your own initiative, following these leads. For example, training manuals and publications of the government agency which employs workers in your field can be useful, particularly for technical and professional positions. A letter or visit to the government department involved may result in more specific study suggestions, and certainly will provide you with a more definite idea of the exact nature of the position you are seeking.

III. KINDS OF TESTS

Tests are used for purposes other than measuring knowledge and ability to perform specified duties. For some positions, it is equally important to test ability to make adjustments to new situations or to profit from training. In others, basic mental abilities not dependent on information are essential. Questions which test these things may not appear as pertinent to the duties of the position as those which test for knowledge and information. Yet they are often highly important parts of a fair examination. For very general questions, it is almost impossible to help you direct your study efforts. What we can do is to point out some of the more common of these general abilities needed in public service positions and describe some typical questions.

1) General information

Broad, general information has been found useful for predicting job success in some kinds of work. This is tested in a variety of ways, from vocabulary lists to questions about current events. Basic background in some field of work, such as sociology or economics, may be sampled in a group of questions. Often these are principles which have become familiar to most persons through exposure rather than through formal training. It is difficult to advise you how to study for these questions; being alert to the world around you is our best suggestion.

2) Verbal ability

An example of an ability needed in many positions is verbal or language ability. Verbal ability is, in brief, the ability to use and understand words. Vocabulary and grammar tests are typical measures of this ability. Reading comprehension or paragraph interpretation questions are common in many kinds of civil service tests. You are given a paragraph of written material and asked to find its central meaning.

3) Numerical ability

Number skills can be tested by the familiar arithmetic problem, by checking paired lists of numbers to see which are alike and which are different, or by interpreting charts and graphs. In the latter test, a graph may be printed in the test booklet which you are asked to use as the basis for answering questions.

4) Observation

A popular test for law-enforcement positions is the observation test. A picture is shown to you for several minutes, then taken away. Questions about the picture test your ability to observe both details and larger elements.

5) Following directions

In many positions in the public service, the employee must be able to carry out written instructions dependably and accurately. You may be given a chart with several columns, each column listing a variety of information. The questions require you to carry out directions involving the information given in the chart.

6) Skills and aptitudes

Performance tests effectively measure some manual skills and aptitudes. When the skill is one in which you are trained, such as typing or shorthand, you can practice. These tests are often very much like those given in business school or high school courses. For many of the other skills and aptitudes, however, no short-time preparation can be made. Skills and abilities natural to you or that you have developed throughout your lifetime are being tested.

Many of the general questions just described provide all the data needed to answer the questions and ask you to use your reasoning ability to find the answers. Your best preparation for these tests, as well as for tests of facts and ideas, is to be at your physical and mental best. You, no doubt, have your own methods of getting into an exam-taking mood and keeping "in shape." The next section lists some ideas on this subject.

IV. KINDS OF QUESTIONS

Only rarely is the "essay" question, which you answer in narrative form, used in civil service tests. Civil service tests are usually of the short-answer type. Full instructions for answering these questions will be given to you at the examination. But in case this is your first experience with short-answer questions and separate answer sheets, here is what you need to know:

1) Multiple-choice Questions

Most popular of the short-answer questions is the "multiple choice" or "best answer" question. It can be used, for example, to test for factual knowledge, ability to solve problems or judgment in meeting situations found at work.

A multiple-choice question is normally one of three types—

- It can begin with an incomplete statement followed by several possible endings. You are to find the one ending which *best* completes the statement, although some of the others may not be entirely wrong.
- It can also be a complete statement in the form of a question which is answered by choosing one of the statements listed.
- It can be in the form of a problem – again you select the best answer.

Here is an example of a multiple-choice question with a discussion which should give you some clues as to the method for choosing the right answer:

When an employee has a complaint about his assignment, the action which will *best* help him overcome his difficulty is to
- A. discuss his difficulty with his coworkers
- B. take the problem to the head of the organization
- C. take the problem to the person who gave him the assignment
- D. say nothing to anyone about his complaint

In answering this question, you should study each of the choices to find which is best. Consider choice "A" – Certainly an employee may discuss his complaint with fellow employees, but no change or improvement can result, and the complaint remains unresolved. Choice "B" is a poor choice since the head of the organization probably does not know what assignment you have been given, and taking your problem to him is known as "going over the head" of the supervisor. The supervisor, or person who made the assignment, is the person who can clarify it or correct any injustice. Choice "C" is, therefore, correct. To say nothing, as in choice "D," is unwise. Supervisors have and interest in knowing the problems employees are facing, and the employee is seeking a solution to his problem.

2) True/False Questions

The "true/false" or "right/wrong" form of question is sometimes used. Here a complete statement is given. Your job is to decide whether the statement is right or wrong.

SAMPLE: A person-to-person long-distance telephone call costs less than a station-to-station call to the same city.

This statement is wrong, or false, since person-to-person calls are more expensive.

This is not a complete list of all possible question forms, although most of the others are variations of these common types. You will always get complete directions for answering questions. Be sure you understand *how* to mark your answers – ask questions until you do.

V. RECORDING YOUR ANSWERS

For an examination with very few applicants, you may be told to record your answers in the test booklet itself. Separate answer sheets are much more common. If this separate answer sheet is to be scored by machine – and this is often the case – it is highly important that you mark your answers correctly in order to get credit.

An electric scoring machine is often used in civil service offices because of the speed with which papers can be scored. Machine-scored answer sheets must be marked with a pencil, which will be given to you. This pencil has a high graphite content which responds to the electric scoring machine. As a matter of fact, stray dots may register as answers, so do not let your pencil rest on the answer sheet while you are pondering the correct answer. Also, if your pencil lead breaks or is otherwise defective, ask for another.

Since the answer sheet will be dropped in a slot in the scoring machine, be careful not to bend the corners or get the paper crumpled.

The answer sheet normally has five vertical columns of numbers, with 30 numbers to a column. These numbers correspond to the question numbers in your test booklet. After each number, going across the page are four or five pairs of dotted lines. These short dotted lines have small letters or numbers above them. The first two pairs may also have a "T" or "F" above the letters. This indicates that the first two pairs only are to be used if the questions are of the true-false type. If the questions are multiple choice, disregard the "T" and "F" and pay attention only to the small letters or numbers.

Answer your questions in the manner of the sample that follows:

32. The largest city in the United States is
   A. Washington, D.C.
   B. New York City
   C. Chicago
   D. Detroit
   E. San Francisco

1) Choose the answer you think is best. (New York City is the largest, so "B" is correct.)
2) Find the row of dotted lines numbered the same as the question you are answering. (Find row number 32)
3) Find the pair of dotted lines corresponding to the answer. (Find the pair of lines under the mark "B.")
4) Make a solid black mark between the dotted lines.

VI. BEFORE THE TEST

Common sense will help you find procedures to follow to get ready for an examination. Too many of us, however, overlook these sensible measures. Indeed, nervousness and fatigue have been found to be the most serious reasons why applicants fail to do their best on civil service tests. Here is a list of reminders:

- Begin your preparation early – Don't wait until the last minute to go scurrying around for books and materials or to find out what the position is all about.
- Prepare continuously – An hour a night for a week is better than an all-night cram session. This has been definitely established. What is more, a night a

week for a month will return better dividends than crowding your study into a shorter period of time.

- Locate the place of the exam – You have been sent a notice telling you when and where to report for the examination. If the location is in a different town or otherwise unfamiliar to you, it would be well to inquire the best route and learn something about the building.
- Relax the night before the test – Allow your mind to rest. Do not study at all that night. Plan some mild recreation or diversion; then go to bed early and get a good night's sleep.
- Get up early enough to make a leisurely trip to the place for the test – This way unforeseen events, traffic snarls, unfamiliar buildings, etc. will not upset you.
- Dress comfortably – A written test is not a fashion show. You will be known by number and not by name, so wear something comfortable.
- Leave excess paraphernalia at home – Shopping bags and odd bundles will get in your way. You need bring only the items mentioned in the official notice you received; usually everything you need is provided. Do not bring reference books to the exam. They will only confuse those last minutes and be taken away from you when in the test room.
- Arrive somewhat ahead of time – If because of transportation schedules you must get there very early, bring a newspaper or magazine to take your mind off yourself while waiting.
- Locate the examination room – When you have found the proper room, you will be directed to the seat or part of the room where you will sit. Sometimes you are given a sheet of instructions to read while you are waiting. Do not fill out any forms until you are told to do so; just read them and be prepared.
- Relax and prepare to listen to the instructions
- If you have any physical problem that may keep you from doing your best, be sure to tell the test administrator. If you are sick or in poor health, you really cannot do your best on the exam. You can come back and take the test some other time.

VII. AT THE TEST

The day of the test is here and you have the test booklet in your hand. The temptation to get going is very strong. Caution! There is more to success than knowing the right answers. You must know how to identify your papers and understand variations in the type of short-answer question used in this particular examination. Follow these suggestions for maximum results from your efforts:

1) Cooperate with the monitor
The test administrator has a duty to create a situation in which you can be as much at ease as possible. He will give instructions, tell you when to begin, check to see that you are marking your answer sheet correctly, and so on. He is not there to guard you, although he will see that your competitors do not take unfair advantage. He wants to help you do your best.

2) Listen to all instructions
Don't jump the gun! Wait until you understand all directions. In most civil service tests you get more time than you need to answer the questions. So don't be in a hurry.

Read each word of instructions until you clearly understand the meaning. Study the examples, listen to all announcements and follow directions. Ask questions if you do not understand what to do.

3) Identify your papers

Civil service exams are usually identified by number only. You will be assigned a number; you must not put your name on your test papers. Be sure to copy your number correctly. Since more than one exam may be given, copy your exact examination title.

4) Plan your time

Unless you are told that a test is a "speed" or "rate of work" test, speed itself is usually not important. Time enough to answer all the questions will be provided, but this does not mean that you have all day. An overall time limit has been set. Divide the total time (in minutes) by the number of questions to determine the approximate time you have for each question.

5) Do not linger over difficult questions

If you come across a difficult question, mark it with a paper clip (useful to have along) and come back to it when you have been through the booklet. One caution if you do this – be sure to skip a number on your answer sheet as well. Check often to be sure that you have not lost your place and that you are marking in the row numbered the same as the question you are answering.

6) Read the questions

Be sure you know what the question asks! Many capable people are unsuccessful because they failed to *read* the questions correctly.

7) Answer all questions

Unless you have been instructed that a penalty will be deducted for incorrect answers, it is better to guess than to omit a question.

8) Speed tests

It is often better NOT to guess on speed tests. It has been found that on timed tests people are tempted to spend the last few seconds before time is called in marking answers at random – without even reading them – in the hope of picking up a few extra points. To discourage this practice, the instructions may warn you that your score will be "corrected" for guessing. That is, a penalty will be applied. The incorrect answers will be deducted from the correct ones, or some other penalty formula will be used.

9) Review your answers

If you finish before time is called, go back to the questions you guessed or omitted to give them further thought. Review other answers if you have time.

10) Return your test materials

If you are ready to leave before others have finished or time is called, take ALL your materials to the monitor and leave quietly. Never take any test material with you. The monitor can discover whose papers are not complete, and taking a test booklet may be grounds for disqualification.

VIII. EXAMINATION TECHNIQUES

1) Read the general instructions carefully. These are usually printed on the first page of the exam booklet. As a rule, these instructions refer to the timing of the examination; the fact that you should not start work until the signal and must stop work at a signal, etc. If there are any *special* instructions, such as a choice of questions to be answered, make sure that you note this instruction carefully.

2) When you are ready to start work on the examination, that is as soon as the signal has been given, read the instructions to each question booklet, underline any key words or phrases, such as *least, best, outline, describe* and the like. In this way you will tend to answer as requested rather than discover on reviewing your paper that you *listed without describing*, that you selected the *worst* choice rather than the *best* choice, etc.

3) If the examination is of the objective or multiple-choice type – that is, each question will also give a series of possible answers: A, B, C or D, and you are called upon to select the best answer and write the letter next to that answer on your answer paper – it is advisable to start answering each question in turn. There may be anywhere from 50 to 100 such questions in the three or four hours allotted and you can see how much time would be taken if you read through all the questions before beginning to answer any. Furthermore, if you come across a question or group of questions which you know would be difficult to answer, it would undoubtedly affect your handling of all the other questions.

4) If the examination is of the essay type and contains but a few questions, it is a moot point as to whether you should read all the questions before starting to answer any one. Of course, if you are given a choice – say five out of seven and the like – then it is essential to read all the questions so you can eliminate the two that are most difficult. If, however, you are asked to answer all the questions, there may be danger in trying to answer the easiest one first because you may find that you will spend too much time on it. The best technique is to answer the first question, then proceed to the second, etc.

5) Time your answers. Before the exam begins, write down the time it started, then add the time allowed for the examination and write down the time it must be completed, then divide the time available somewhat as follows:
   - If 3-1/2 hours are allowed, that would be 210 minutes. If you have 80 objective-type questions, that would be an average of 2-1/2 minutes per question. Allow yourself no more than 2 minutes per question, or a total of 160 minutes, which will permit about 50 minutes to review.
   - If for the time allotment of 210 minutes there are 7 essay questions to answer, that would average about 30 minutes a question. Give yourself only 25 minutes per question so that you have about 35 minutes to review.

6) The most important instruction is to *read each question* and make sure you know what is wanted. The second most important instruction is to *time yourself properly* so that you answer every question. The third most

important instruction is to *answer every question*. Guess if you have to but include something for each question. Remember that you will receive no credit for a blank and will probably receive some credit if you write something in answer to an essay question. If you guess a letter – say "B" for a multiple-choice question – you may have guessed right. If you leave a blank as an answer to a multiple-choice question, the examiners may respect your feelings but it will not add a point to your score. Some exams may penalize you for wrong answers, so in such cases *only*, you may not want to guess unless you have some basis for your answer.

7) Suggestions
   a. Objective-type questions
      1. Examine the question booklet for proper sequence of pages and questions
      2. Read all instructions carefully
      3. Skip any question which seems too difficult; return to it after all other questions have been answered
      4. Apportion your time properly; do not spend too much time on any single question or group of questions
      5. Note and underline key words – *all, most, fewest, least, best, worst, same, opposite,* etc.
      6. Pay particular attention to negatives
      7. Note unusual option, e.g., unduly long, short, complex, different or similar in content to the body of the question
      8. Observe the use of "hedging" words – *probably, may, most likely,* etc.
      9. Make sure that your answer is put next to the same number as the question
      10. Do not second-guess unless you have good reason to believe the second answer is definitely more correct
      11. Cross out original answer if you decide another answer is more accurate; do not erase until you are ready to hand your paper in
      12. Answer all questions; guess unless instructed otherwise
      13. Leave time for review

   b. Essay questions
      1. Read each question carefully
      2. Determine exactly what is wanted. Underline key words or phrases.
      3. Decide on outline or paragraph answer
      4. Include many different points and elements unless asked to develop any one or two points or elements
      5. Show impartiality by giving pros and cons unless directed to select one side only
      6. Make and write down any assumptions you find necessary to answer the questions
      7. Watch your English, grammar, punctuation and choice of words
      8. Time your answers; don't crowd material

8) Answering the essay question

Most essay questions can be answered by framing the specific response around several key words or ideas. Here are a few such key words or ideas:

M's: manpower, materials, methods, money, management
P's: purpose, program, policy, plan, procedure, practice, problems, pitfalls, personnel, public relations
  a. Six basic steps in handling problems:
     1. Preliminary plan and background development
     2. Collect information, data and facts
     3. Analyze and interpret information, data and facts
     4. Analyze and develop solutions as well as make recommendations
     5. Prepare report and sell recommendations
     6. Install recommendations and follow up effectiveness

  b. Pitfalls to avoid
     1. *Taking things for granted* – A statement of the situation does not necessarily imply that each of the elements is necessarily true; for example, a complaint may be invalid and biased so that all that can be taken for granted is that a complaint has been registered
     2. *Considering only one side of a situation* – Wherever possible, indicate several alternatives and then point out the reasons you selected the best one
     3. *Failing to indicate follow up* – Whenever your answer indicates action on your part, make certain that you will take proper follow-up action to see how successful your recommendations, procedures or actions turn out to be
     4. *Taking too long in answering any single question* – Remember to time your answers properly

IX. AFTER THE TEST

     Scoring procedures differ in detail among civil service jurisdictions although the general principles are the same. Whether the papers are hand-scored or graded by machine we have described, they are nearly always graded by number. That is, the person who marks the paper knows only the number – never the name – of the applicant. Not until all the papers have been graded will they be matched with names. If other tests, such as training and experience or oral interview ratings have been given, scores will be combined. Different parts of the examination usually have different weights. For example, the written test might count 60 percent of the final grade, and a rating of training and experience 40 percent. In many jurisdictions, veterans will have a certain number of points added to their grades.
     After the final grade has been determined, the names are placed in grade order and an eligible list is established. There are various methods for resolving ties between those who get the same final grade – probably the most common is to place first the name of the person whose application was received first. Job offers are made from the eligible list in the order the names appear on it. You will be notified of your grade and your rank as soon as all these computations have been made. This will be done as rapidly as possible.
     People who are found to meet the requirements in the announcement are called "eligibles." Their names are put on a list of eligible candidates. An eligible's chances of getting a job depend on how high he stands on this list and how fast agencies are filling jobs from the list.

When a job is to be filled from a list of eligibles, the agency asks for the names of people on the list of eligibles for that job. When the civil service commission receives this request, it sends to the agency the names of the three people highest on this list. Or, if the job to be filled has specialized requirements, the office sends the agency the names of the top three persons who meet these requirements from the general list.

The appointing officer makes a choice from among the three people whose names were sent to him. If the selected person accepts the appointment, the names of the others are put back on the list to be considered for future openings.

That is the rule in hiring from all kinds of eligible lists, whether they are for typist, carpenter, chemist, or something else. For every vacancy, the appointing officer has his choice of any one of the top three eligibles on the list. This explains why the person whose name is on top of the list sometimes does not get an appointment when some of the persons lower on the list do. If the appointing officer chooses the second or third eligible, the No. 1 eligible does not get a job at once, but stays on the list until he is appointed or the list is terminated.

X. HOW TO PASS THE INTERVIEW TEST

The examination for which you applied requires an oral interview test. You have already taken the written test and you are now being called for the interview test – the final part of the formal examination.

You may think that it is not possible to prepare for an interview test and that there are no procedures to follow during an interview. Our purpose is to point out some things you can do in advance that will help you and some good rules to follow and pitfalls to avoid while you are being interviewed.

What is an interview supposed to test?

The written examination is designed to test the technical knowledge and competence of the candidate; the oral is designed to evaluate intangible qualities, not readily measured otherwise, and to establish a list showing the relative fitness of each candidate – as measured against his competitors – for the position sought. Scoring is not on the basis of "right" and "wrong," but on a sliding scale of values ranging from "not passable" to "outstanding." As a matter of fact, it is possible to achieve a relatively low score without a single "incorrect" answer because of evident weakness in the qualities being measured.

Occasionally, an examination may consist entirely of an oral test – either an individual or a group oral. In such cases, information is sought concerning the technical knowledges and abilities of the candidate, since there has been no written examination for this purpose. More commonly, however, an oral test is used to supplement a written examination.

Who conducts interviews?

The composition of oral boards varies among different jurisdictions. In nearly all, a representative of the personnel department serves as chairman. One of the members of the board may be a representative of the department in which the candidate would work. In some cases, "outside experts" are used, and, frequently, a businessman or some other representative of the general public is asked to serve. Labor and management or other special groups may be represented. The aim is to secure the services of experts in the appropriate field.

However the board is composed, it is a good idea (and not at all improper or unethical) to ascertain in advance of the interview who the members are and what groups they represent. When you are introduced to them, you will have some idea of their backgrounds and interests, and at least you will not stutter and stammer over their names.

What should be done before the interview?

While knowledge about the board members is useful and takes some of the surprise element out of the interview, there is other preparation which is more substantive. It *is* possible to prepare for an oral interview – in several ways:

1) Keep a copy of your application and review it carefully before the interview

This may be the only document before the oral board, and the starting point of the interview. Know what education and experience you have listed there, and the sequence and dates of all of it. Sometimes the board will ask you to review the highlights of your experience for them; you should not have to hem and haw doing it.

2) Study the class specification and the examination announcement

Usually, the oral board has one or both of these to guide them. The qualities, characteristics or knowledges required by the position sought are stated in these documents. They offer valuable clues as to the nature of the oral interview. For example, if the job involves supervisory responsibilities, the announcement will usually indicate that knowledge of modern supervisory methods and the qualifications of the candidate as a supervisor will be tested. If so, you can expect such questions, frequently in the form of a hypothetical situation which you are expected to solve. NEVER go into an oral without knowledge of the duties and responsibilities of the job you seek.

3) Think through each qualification required

Try to visualize the kind of questions you would ask if you were a board member. How well could you answer them? Try especially to appraise your own knowledge and background in each area, *measured against the job sought*, and identify any areas in which you are weak. Be critical and realistic – do not flatter yourself.

4) Do some general reading in areas in which you feel you may be weak

For example, if the job involves supervision and your past experience has NOT, some general reading in supervisory methods and practices, particularly in the field of human relations, might be useful. Do NOT study agency procedures or detailed manuals. The oral board will be testing your understanding and capacity, not your memory.

5) Get a good night's sleep and watch your general health and mental attitude

You will want a clear head at the interview. Take care of a cold or any other minor ailment, and of course, no hangovers.

What should be done on the day of the interview?

Now comes the day of the interview itself. Give yourself plenty of time to get there. Plan to arrive somewhat ahead of the scheduled time, particularly if your appointment is in the fore part of the day. If a previous candidate fails to appear, the board might be ready for you a bit early. By early afternoon an oral board is almost invariably behind schedule if there are many candidates, and you may have to wait.

Take along a book or magazine to read, or your application to review, but leave any extraneous material in the waiting room when you go in for your interview. In any event, relax and compose yourself.

The matter of dress is important. The board is forming impressions about you – from your experience, your manners, your attitude, and your appearance. Give your personal appearance careful attention. Dress your best, but not your flashiest. Choose conservative, appropriate clothing, and be sure it is immaculate. This is a business interview, and your appearance should indicate that you regard it as such. Besides, being well groomed and properly dressed will help boost your confidence.

Sooner or later, someone will call your name and escort you into the interview room. *This is it.* From here on you are on your own. It is too late for any more preparation. But remember, you asked for this opportunity to prove your fitness, and you are here because your request was granted.

What happens when you go in?

The usual sequence of events will be as follows: The clerk (who is often the board stenographer) will introduce you to the chairman of the oral board, who will introduce you to the other members of the board. Acknowledge the introductions before you sit down. Do not be surprised if you find a microphone facing you or a stenotypist sitting by. Oral interviews are usually recorded in the event of an appeal or other review.

Usually the chairman of the board will open the interview by reviewing the highlights of your education and work experience from your application – primarily for the benefit of the other members of the board, as well as to get the material into the record. Do not interrupt or comment unless there is an error or significant misinterpretation; if that is the case, do not hesitate. But do not quibble about insignificant matters. Also, he will usually ask you some question about your education, experience or your present job – partly to get you to start talking and to establish the interviewing "rapport." He may start the actual questioning, or turn it over to one of the other members. Frequently, each member undertakes the questioning on a particular area, one in which he is perhaps most competent, so you can expect each member to participate in the examination. Because time is limited, you may also expect some rather abrupt switches in the direction the questioning takes, so do not be upset by it. Normally, a board member will not pursue a single line of questioning unless he discovers a particular strength or weakness.

After each member has participated, the chairman will usually ask whether any member has any further questions, then will ask you if you have anything you wish to add. Unless you are expecting this question, it may floor you. Worse, it may start you off on an extended, extemporaneous speech. The board is not usually seeking more information. The question is principally to offer you a last opportunity to present further qualifications or to indicate that you have nothing to add. So, if you feel that a significant qualification or characteristic has been overlooked, it is proper to point it out in a sentence or so. Do not compliment the board on the thoroughness of their examination – they have been sketchy, and you know it. If you wish, merely say, "No thank you, I have nothing further to add." This is a point where you can "talk yourself out" of a good impression or fail to present an important bit of information. Remember, *you close the interview yourself.*

The chairman will then say, "That is all, Mr. _____, thank you." Do not be startled; the interview is over, and quicker than you think. Thank him, gather your belongings and take your leave. Save your sigh of relief for the other side of the door.

How to put your best foot forward

Throughout this entire process, you may feel that the board individually and collectively is trying to pierce your defenses, seek out your hidden weaknesses and embarrass and confuse you. Actually, this is not true. They are obliged to make an appraisal of your qualifications for the job you are seeking, and they want to see you in your best light. Remember, they must interview all candidates and a non-cooperative candidate may become a failure in spite of their best efforts to bring out his qualifications. Here are 15 suggestions that will help you:

1) Be natural – Keep your attitude confident, not cocky

If you are not confident that you can do the job, do not expect the board to be. Do not apologize for your weaknesses, try to bring out your strong points. The board is interested in a positive, not negative, presentation. Cockiness will antagonize any board member and make him wonder if you are covering up a weakness by a false show of strength.

2) Get comfortable, but don't lounge or sprawl

Sit erectly but not stiffly. A careless posture may lead the board to conclude that you are careless in other things, or at least that you are not impressed by the importance of the occasion. Either conclusion is natural, even if incorrect. Do not fuss with your clothing, a pencil or an ashtray. Your hands may occasionally be useful to emphasize a point; do not let them become a point of distraction.

3) Do not wisecrack or make small talk

This is a serious situation, and your attitude should show that you consider it as such. Further, the time of the board is limited – they do not want to waste it, and neither should you.

4) Do not exaggerate your experience or abilities

In the first place, from information in the application or other interviews and sources, the board may know more about you than you think. Secondly, you probably will not get away with it. An experienced board is rather adept at spotting such a situation, so do not take the chance.

5) If you know a board member, do not make a point of it, yet do not hide it

Certainly you are not fooling him, and probably not the other members of the board. Do not try to take advantage of your acquaintanceship – it will probably do you little good.

6) Do not dominate the interview

Let the board do that. They will give you the clues – do not assume that you have to do all the talking. Realize that the board has a number of questions to ask you, and do not try to take up all the interview time by showing off your extensive knowledge of the answer to the first one.

7) Be attentive

You only have 20 minutes or so, and you should keep your attention at its sharpest throughout. When a member is addressing a problem or question to you, give him your undivided attention. Address your reply principally to him, but do not exclude the other board members.

8) Do not interrupt

A board member may be stating a problem for you to analyze. He will ask you a question when the time comes. Let him state the problem, and wait for the question.

9) Make sure you understand the question

Do not try to answer until you are sure what the question is. If it is not clear, restate it in your own words or ask the board member to clarify it for you. However, do not haggle about minor elements.

10) Reply promptly but not hastily

A common entry on oral board rating sheets is "candidate responded readily," or "candidate hesitated in replies." Respond as promptly and quickly as you can, but do not jump to a hasty, ill-considered answer.

11) Do not be peremptory in your answers

A brief answer is proper – but do not fire your answer back. That is a losing game from your point of view. The board member can probably ask questions much faster than you can answer them.

12) Do not try to create the answer you think the board member wants

He is interested in what kind of mind you have and how it works – not in playing games. Furthermore, he can usually spot this practice and will actually grade you down on it.

13) Do not switch sides in your reply merely to agree with a board member

Frequently, a member will take a contrary position merely to draw you out and to see if you are willing and able to defend your point of view. Do not start a debate, yet do not surrender a good position. If a position is worth taking, it is worth defending.

14) Do not be afraid to admit an error in judgment if you are shown to be wrong

The board knows that you are forced to reply without any opportunity for careful consideration. Your answer may be demonstrably wrong. If so, admit it and get on with the interview.

15) Do not dwell at length on your present job

The opening question may relate to your present assignment. Answer the question but do not go into an extended discussion. You are being examined for a *new* job, not your present one. As a matter of fact, try to phrase ALL your answers in terms of the job for which you are being examined.

Basis of Rating

Probably you will forget most of these "do's" and "don'ts" when you walk into the oral interview room. Even remembering them all will not ensure you a passing grade. Perhaps you did not have the qualifications in the first place. But remembering them will help you to put your best foot forward, without treading on the toes of the board members.

Rumor and popular opinion to the contrary notwithstanding, an oral board wants you to make the best appearance possible. They know you are under pressure – but they also want to see how you respond to it as a guide to what your reaction would be under the pressures of the job you seek. They will be influenced by the degree of poise you display, the personal traits you show and the manner in which you respond.

EXAMINATION SECTION

EXAMINATION SECTION
TEST 1

DIRECTIONS: Each question or incomplete statement is followed by several suggested answers or completions. Select the one that BEST answers the question or completes the statement. *PRINT THE LETTER OF THE CORRECT ANSWER IN THE SPACE AT THE RIGHT.*

1. Which of the following natural resources is classified as inexhaustible/immutable, or incapable of much change or alteration through human activity?   1____

    A.   Agricultural products
    B.   Atomic energy
    C.   Waterpower of flowing streams
    D.   Mineral resources

2. Each of the following practices is a current method for maintaining the utility of cattle grazing rangeland EXCEPT   2____

    A.   manipulating stock herds
    B.   reseeding
    C.   firing
    D.   maintaining constant grazing pressure

3. The one of the following considered to be an ADVANTAGE of monocultural forest harvesting is   3____

    A.   superior wood quality
    B.   makes use of built-in ecological balancing mechanisms
    C.   allows nurturing of shade-intolerant species
    D.   decreased susceptibility to fires

4. The type of soil that is BEST able to hold water is   4____

    A.   silt   B.   sandy clay
    C.   silty clay   D.   loam

5. The practice of *chipping, or* breaking the forest harvest down into smaller particles that can be compressed into useful products, can INCREASE the forest yield by _____ %.   5____

    A.   25   B.   50   C.   100   D.   200

6. The _____ industry generates the MOST revenue in the United States.   6____

    A.   steel   B.   cattle
    C.   textiles   D.   automobile

7. Which of the following is NOT considered to be a guiding principle in the current model for conserving natural resources?   7____

    A.   Balancing individual privilege with individual responsibility
    B.   Ultimate government control of conservation efforts
    C.   Concentrated, singular use of particular resources
    D.   Frequent inventory and projection of resource use

8. One of soil's macronutrients is 8___

   A. cobalt   B. calcium   C. zinc   D. copper

9. Food production in the United States is currently hindered by all of the following factors EXCEPT the 9___

   A. loss of farmland to land development
   B. gradually increasing average temperatures
   C. huge fossil fuel input requirement for production
   D. transfer of water to urban populations

10. The bark of trees, long discarded as useless by loggers, has proven to be a useful resource for all of the following purposes EXCEPT 10___

   A. medical uses
   B. construction of building frames
   C. production of chemicals for tanning leather
   D. oil-well drilling compounds

11. Of the following, the one that is NOT generally considered to be an advantage associated with the use of organic fertilizers is 11___

   A. increased rate of water release
   B. prevention of leaching
   C. improved soil structure
   D. maximum aeration of root zone

12. APPROXIMATELY _____ percent of the earth's freshwater supply is underground. 12___

   A. 30   B. 50   C. 75   D. 95

13. Which of the following is NOT generally considered to be part of the ocean's contribution as a natural resource? 13___
A

   A. highway for international transport
   B. replenisher of oxygen supply through algeal photosynthesis
   C. major source of important vitamins in the human diet
   D. major source of important proteins in the human diet

14. The natural resource GENERALLY considered to be inexhaustible, but whose quality can be impaired by misuse, is 14___

   A. rangeland   B. marine fish and mammals
   C. static mineral resources   D. solar energy

15. The one of the following resources that can be converted into methane gas by high-pressure steam heating is 15___

   A. high-sulfur coal
   B. solid animal wastes
   C. petroleum
   D. human garbage and solid wastes

16. Given the current methods of using fossil fuels, the LEAST defensible (most wasteful), according to scientists, is   16____

    A. synthetic or bacterial food production
    B. heating
    C. petrochemicals
    D. synthetic polymers

17. The BEST way to restore soil fertility is by   17____

    A. organic fertilizers   B. inorganic fertilizers
    C. crop rotation   D. strip cropping

18. The MINIMUM amount of time that toxic material will remain in a given groundwater supply is generally considered to be _____ years.   18____

    A. 10   B. 30   C. 200   D. 1,000

19. What is considered to be the MOST influential factor governing the occurrence and behavior of aquatic life?   19____

    A. Availability of food   B. Availability of sunlight
    C. Availability of oxygen   D. Temperature

20. Which of the following has NOT proven to be a consequence involved in the use of solar energy?   20____

    A. Toxicity of working fluids
    B. Decrease in photosynthetic rates of surrounding flora
    C. Climatic change
    D. Marine pollution

21. More than 50% of the coal that has ever been mined from the earth has been extracted in the last years.   21____

    A. 100   B. 50   C. 25   D. 10

22. The natural resource classified as exhaustible but renewable, meaning that its permanence is dependent on how it is used by humans, is   22____

    A. fossil fuels   B. wildlife species
    C. solar energy   D. soil

23. The one of the following that is NOT a limiting power held by the International Whaling Commission over commercial whalers is   23____

    A. protecting certain species
    B. deciding minimum length for permissible kill
    C. protecting breeding grounds
    D. protecting calves and nursing cows

24. Which of the following is generally accepted as the MOST promising solution to the increasing worldwide food shortage?   24____

    A. Development of more effective fertilizers
    B. Vigorous human population control
    C. More efficient pest control
    D. Decreased reliance on meat as a food source

25. The contaminants PRIMARILY responsible for the depletion of the earth's atmospheric ozone are   25____

    A. carbon monoxide   B. chlorinated fluorocarbons
    C. dioxins   D. steam

KEY (CORRECT ANSWERS)

1.	B		11.	A
2.	D		12.	D
3.	C		13.	C
4.	B		14.	D
5.	D		15.	A
6.	B		16.	B
7.	C		17.	A
8.	B		18.	C
9.	B		19.	D
10.	B		20.	B

21.	C
22.	D
23.	C
24.	B
25.	B

TEST 2

DIRECTIONS: Each question or incomplete statement is followed by several suggested answers or completions. Select the one that BEST answers the question or completes the statement. *PRINT THE LETTER OF THE CORRECT ANSWER IN THE SPACE AT THE RIGHT.*

1. Which of the following is currently the MOST promising method for the management of the earth's wildlife resources?   1____

    A.   Introduction of exotics   B.   B. Habitat development
    C.   Predator control   D.   Game laws

2. The element of American society that is MOST responsible for consuming the largest share of energy resources is   2____

    A.   industry   B.   home construction
    C.   transportation   D.   recreation

3. Of all the water drawn and transported for irrigation purposes in the United States, APPROXIMATELY _____ percent is eventually absorbed by the root systems of crops.   3____

    A.   10   B.   25   C.   50   D.   75

4. The APPROXIMATE rate at which the Mississippi River currently carries topsoil into the Gulf of Mexico is _____ tons per _____.   4____

    A.   thirty; minute   B.   one hundred; minute
    C.   fifteen; second   D.   fifty; hour

5. According to current projections, it will be approximately _____ years before the world's fossil fuel resources are completely exhausted, given current methods of use.   5____

    A.   thirty-five   B.   fifty
    C.   seventy-five   D.   one hundred

6. Each of the following is considered to be a disadvantage to monocultural systems for forest harvesting EXCEPT   6____

    A.   long harvesting rotations
    B.   inefficiency in growing and harvesting large crops
    C.   runoff from intensive chemical use
    D.   creation of oversimplified ecosystems

7. _____ is considered to be among soil's micronutrients.   7____

    A.   Manganese   B.   Nitrate
    C.   Potassium   D.   Calcium

8. In relation to the population growth of the United States, what is the increase in per capita rate energy consumption? It is increasing at about _____ rate of population growth.   8____

    A.   half the   B.   the same
    C.   twice the   D.   five times the

9. Which of the following is NOT considered to be a disadvantage associated with the dam-   9___
ming of flowing streams and rivers?

    A. Decreased energy potential
    B. Increased flooding
    C. Sedimentation of reservoirs
    D. Complications with the irrigating process

10. Given the topography of most United States farmland, the one of the following which has   10___
NOT proven an efficient method for the control of soil erosion by water is

    A. contour farming   B. gully reclamation
    C. terracing   D. planting shelterbelts

11. Of the following natural resources, the one classified as a consumptively used resource,   11___
or one whose eventual exhaustion is CERTAIN given current use patterns, is

    A. gem minerals   B. freshwater fish
    C. stationary water sources   D. natural gas

12. In forestry, a sustained-yield harvest program, one that produces a moderate crop that   12___
can be harvested year after year, is called

    A. silvicultural   B. clear-cutting
    C. agricultural   D. monocultural

13. Approximately _____ tons of soil are washed away ANNUALLY from the United States.   13___

    A. fourteen million   B. fifty-five million
    C. one billion   D. three billion

14. Each of the following is considered to be a disadvantage associated with *channelization*,   14___
or the artificial widening of rivers and streams, EXCEPT

    A. loss of hardwood timber
    B. loss of wildlife habitat
    C. lowering of water table
    D. increased flood risk

15. The MOST defensible (least wasteful) use of aquifer water, according to most current sci-   15___
entists, is to

    A. irrigate monocultural crop systems
    B. relieve drought
    C. provide for industrial cleaning processes
    D. fill existing reservoirs

16. Given the current methods of using fossil fuels, the MOST defensible (least wasteful)   16___
one, according to scientists, is

    A. essential liquid fuels   B. heating
    C. industrial purposes   D. electricity

17. The annual allotment of acres of _____ rangeland per head is considered to be universally standard for a single cattle animal's grazing.   17____

   A. two   B. four   C. eight   D. twelve

18. APPROXIMATELY _____ percent of the extracted forest product in the United States is used for lumber.   18____

   A. 30   B. 50   C. 70   D. 95

19. _____ is NOT considered to be an influential factor in the depletion of American soil nutrients.   19____

   A. Cropping   B. Erosion
   C. Pesticide use   D. Fertilization

20. Which of the following is NOT considered to be a factor contributing to the decline of our freshwater fish resources?   20____

   A. Decreasing habitat temperatures
   B. Toxic industrial waste
   C. Oxygen depletion
   D. Siltation

21. Of the following uses of a metallic natural resource, the one which is NOT generally considered to be consumptive or exhausting is   21____

   A. zinc in galvanized iron
   B. tin in toothpaste tubes
   C. aluminum in cans and containers
   D. lead in gasoline

22. Each of the following is an effect of oil pollution on marine ecosystems EXCEPT   22____

   A. introduction of carcinogens into food chain
   B. acceleration of photosynthetic rates
   C. concentration of chlorinated hydrocarbons
   D. immediate mortality of marine animals

23. The forestry practice of *clear-cutting* is defensively used in the   23____

   A. old-growth firs of the Pacific Northwest
   B. oak groves throughout the Midwest
   C. sequoia groves of Northern California
   D. pine barrens of New Jersey

24. Each of the following is a factor that affects the erosion of soil by water EXCEPT   24____

   A. volume of precipitation
   B. wind patterns
   C. topography of land
   D. type of vegetational cover

25. Which of the following is classified as an inorganic soil fertilizer?   25____

   A. Legumes   B. Manure   C. Sewage   D. Nitrates

KEY (CORRECT ANSWERS)

1.	B		11.	D
2.	A		12.	A
3.	B		13.	C
4.	C		14.	D
5.	A		15.	B
6.	B		16.	A
7.	A		17.	C
8.	D		18.	A
9.	C		19.	D
10.	C		20.	A

21.	C
22.	B
23.	A
24.	B
25.	D

———————

EXAMINATION SECTION

DIRECTIONS: Each question or incomplete statement is followed by
several suggested answers or completions. Select the
one that BEST answers the question or completes the
statement. *PRINT THE LETTER OF THE CORRECT ANSWER
IN THE SPACE AT THE RIGHT.*

1. Low productivity can often be improved by: 1. ___
   I. Planting a pure stand
   II. Application of organic matter
   III. Application of phosphorus
   IV. Growing a rye crop before establishing a stand
   V. Application of podsolization and more types of humus

   The CORRECT answer is:
   A. I,II,V   B. I,III,V   C. II,III,IV
   D. II,III,IV,V   E. All of the above

2. The extent to which grazing affects the productivity of   2. ___
   forest soil depends on the
   I. season of use   II. type of soil   III. climate
   IV. topography   V. character of trees

   The CORRECT answer is:
   A. II,V   B. I,II,V   C. II,III,IV
   D. All of the above   E. None of the above

3. All of the following contribute to the effects of clear-   3. ___
   cutting EXCEPT
   A. soil texture   B. the character of the precipitation
   C. amount of low vegetation   D. soil structure
   E. aspect

4. *What* ranges are used for yearling grazing?   4. ___
   A. High alpine slopes and meadows
   B. Ranges at intermediate elevations
   C. Sub-alpine herblands of the West
   D. Desert grasslands of the Southwest
   E. Deserts of the Great Basin with certain shrub types

5. All of the following are ways that protective vegetation   5. ___
   favors a more luxuriant population of animals and plants
   EXCEPT: There is
   A. a more equable temperature
   B. less wind on sites with protective vegetation
   C. reduced evaporation loss from the soil
   D. higher atmospheric humidity
   E. increased light intensity

6. *Which* of the following are elements of the range eco-system?   6.
   I. Topography II. Climate   III. Vegetation
   IV. Animals   V. Soil

   The CORRECT answer is:
   A. I,II   B. III,IV   C. I,II,V   D. III,IV,V
   E. All of the above

7. *Which* of the following are true of Primary Successions? The   7.
   change
   A. alters the soil   B. is irreversible
   C. is orderly   D. may destroy the soil
   E. may accelerate soil erosion

   The CORRECT answer is:
   A. I,III   B. I,II,III   C. I,IV,V   D. I,II,IV,V
   E. All of the above

8. All of the following constitute good range usage EXCEPT: 8.
   A. Grazing the kinds of animals that will economically utilize
      forage plants
   B. Concentrating grazing animals on certain parts of ranges
      to leave areas of forage unused
   C. Adjusting the grazing use of each unit seasonally to meet
      growth requirements
   D. Adjusting the numbers of grazing animals to attain an
      intensity of forage use
   E. Adjusting grazing use for uniform use of forage

9. *What* is the purpose of fencing the range into units? It   9.
   A. *makes* deferred grazing practical
   B. *allows* even distribution of livestock
   C. *regulates* the number of grazing animals
   D. *separates* different kinds of grazing animals
   E. *helps* to avoid double use of forage

10. *Which* of the following are effective in controlling undesirable 10.
    species that sprout readily from the roots or stem crowns?
    I. Insects   II. Fire   III. Herbicides
    IV. Grazing   V. Mechanical methods

    The CORRECT answer is:
    A. I,II   B. I,V   C. I,III   D. II,III,IV
    E. All of the above

11. All of the following are ways in which thinning improves growth 11.
    in dense, established stands EXCEPT: Thinning
    A. provides for greater air movement
    B. reduces competition for moisture
    C. decreases competition for nutrients
    D. inhibits decomposition of humus
    E. promotes development of understory vegetation

2

12. Damage due to grazing livestock on forest lands leads to   12. ___
    A. increased layers of friable soil
    B. greater porosity
    C. higher infiltration rates
    D. less water storage in the soil
    E. decreased erosion

13. An *essential* requirement for low-damage logging is: 13. ___
    A. *Providing* channels for surface run-off
    B. *Limiting* skidding to steep slopes
    C. *Laying* roads across slopes
    D. *Underscutting* unstable rock masses
    E. *Using stream* channels as far as possible

14. *How* does pasture management *differ* from range management?   14. ___
    It is concerned with
    A. the improvement of the forage resource
    B. protecting the soil
    C. ecology
    D. soil fertility
    E. maintenance of an adequate ground cover

15. *Which* of the following are interdependent?   15. ___
    A. Cattle and soil   B. Vegetation and soil
    C. Nutrients and soil   D. Insects and soil
    E. Fungi and vegetation

16. When one community of perennials succeeds another until the   16. ___
    original native cover returns on a range site disturbed by
    heavy grazing, it is called
    A. Perennial Succession   B. Primary Succession
    C. Disturbance Succession   D. Restoration
    E. Natural Selection

17. When any material amount of soil is lost from a range site,   17. ___
    replacement
    A. takes place through primary succession
    B. takes place through secondary succession
    C. takes place through natural succession
    D. takes place evolutionally
    E. is not possible

18. If a range area has one predominant class of forage,   18. ___
    A. graze by using one kind of stock
    B. graze with both cattle and sheep
    C. graze the plants before they have much growth
    D. use repeated grazing
    E. use close grazing during the heading and flowering stages

19. *What* are the effects of contour furrowing of rangelands?   19. ___
    It
      I. *helps retain* water
     II. *stimulates* greater growth of forage
    III. *protects* adjacent, low-lying lands from the effects of siltation
     IV. *restores* the infiltration capacity of the soil
      V. *controls* surface run-off

    The CORRECT answer is:
    A. I,III,IV   B. II,IV   C. I,III,V   D. I,II,III
    E. All of the above

3

20. *Which* of the following is *true* of the destruction of un-   20. ___
    desirable plants on the range?
    A. Grazing freshly-burned range is essential
    B. Burning and mechanical methods of destruction should
       take place in late summer or fall
    C. Undesirable species in the understory should be burned
       when the dominant species is destroyed
    D. After the destruction of undesirable plants, they must
       be replaced with something desirable
    E. After the destruction of undesirable plants, natural vege-
       tation should be allowed to develop

21. *What* is the MOST practical way to upgrade soil productivity   21. ___
    in a coniferous monoculture?
    A. Establish a hardwood understory
    B. Prescribe burning
    C. Thin the stand
    D. Establish a legume ground-cover
    E. Establish a mixed coniferous stand

22. *Which* of the following is NOT a benefit of controlled graz-   22. ___
    ing? It
    A. *decreases* the volume of flash fuels
    B. *reduces* the density of ground cover
    C. *favors* establishment of tree reproduction
    D. *curtails* the growth of hardwoods
    E. *breaks down* soil aggregates into finer particles

23. *What* proportion of the forest area may be compacted by log-   23. ___
    ging operations? Up to
    A. 10%   B. 25%   C. 40%   D. 55%   E. 60%

24. *Which* of the following statements is TRUE of ranges?   24. ___
    A. Ranges are seldom dominated by plant species native to the
       site.
    B. Range utilization is larger than pasture utilization.
    C. Erosion is less of a problem on ranges than on pastures.
    D. Ranges have a more luxuriant plant-cover than pastures.
    E. Ranges are generally located in gentler terrains.

25. *What* is the MOST critical element on most Western ranges?   25. ___
    A. Soil moisture   B. Soil texture   C. Topography
    D. Climate   E. Soil fertility

26. *Which* range-grazing animals cause the grasses to diminish   26. ___
    and the broad-leaved plants to increase?
    A. Sheep   B. Cattle   C. Hogs   D. Goats   E. Horses

27. *What* is the Range Manager's FIRST concern?   27. ___
    A. High production of vegetation
    B. Inadequacy of the vegetation
    C. Improving soil fertility
    D. Augmenting the forage resource
    E. Supervision of grazing

4

28. All of the following statements are *true* EXCEPT: Grazing   28. ___
    should be
    A. *slackened* or *prevented* during the heading stage of the plant
    B. *avoided* before the plants have an opportunity to re-
       grow
    C. *shunned* on ranges that naturally support one predominant
       class of forage
    D. *delayed* before plants have begun to manufacture plant foods
    E. *abstained from* in wet-soil conditions

29. Foliage growth is *directly* stimulated by: 29. ___
    I. Burning   II. Range-pitting   III. Contour-furrowing
    IV. Deferred grazing   V. Water-spreading

    The CORRECT answer is:
    A. I,IV,V   B. II,III,IV   C. III,IV,V
    D. All of the above   E. None of the above

30. *What* is the MOST common cause of chlorosis in conifers and   30. ___
    hardwoods?
    A. Lack of water   B. Nitrogen or iron deficiency
    C. Virus   D. Bacteria and fungi
    E. Water deficiencies coupled with root aphids

31. *What* is the result of hardwood litter mixing with coniferous   31. ___
    litter? It
    A. *increases* soil acidity
    B. *reduces* nitrification
    C. *stimulates* decomposition of organic matter
    D. *favors* podsolization
    E. *seals* the soil's pores and provides for slow moisture
       infiltration

32. Moderate grazing is practical in   32. ___
    A. forests after a heavy burn
    B. dense spruce—or hemlock—type forests
    C. open hardwood forests on heavy, fine-textured soils
    D. open-crowned pine forests on sandy soils
    E. any forest with fine-textured soil

33. *Which* of the following may result from clear-cutting?   33. ___
    I. Compaction of soil   II. Reduced rates of infiltration
    III. More water storage   IV. Less surface run-off
    V. Less erosion

    The CORRECT answer is:
    A. I,II   B. II,III,IV,V   C. I,V
    D. All of the above   E. None of the above

34. *What* is the *fundamental* ecological unit of range management?   34. ___
    The
    A. site   B. forage plants   C. ranger
    D. climate   E. grazing resource

35. A *significant* characteristic of most rangelands with a normal 35. __
    plant cover is that
    A. water percolates slowly through the layers of soil
    B. the water table is higher than normal
    C. the surface of the soil is highly permeable to water
    D. compaction is not a factor
    E. erosion is less common than it is on pasture land

36. Slow development of soil and vegetation over the ages is   36. __
    called _____ Succession.
    A. Secondary   B. Disturbance   C. Primary
    D. Natural   E. Perennial

37. *What* is the MAIN reason why plant residues are important in   37. __
    range management? Plant residues
    A. *improve* soil structure
    B. *increase* the aggregation of soil particles
    C. *enlarge* pore space
    D. *protect* the soil
    E. *enhance* the ability of the soil to absorb water

38. Most of the important forage plants can withstand removal   38. __
    of about _____ of the weight of their annual herbage
    production.
    A. 15%   B. 25%   C. 40%   D. 50%   E. 65%

39. All of the following are benefits of seeding rangelands   39. __
    EXCEPT: It
    A. *restores* desirable soil
    B. *rebuilds* site conditions on disturbed areas
    C. *increases* grazing capacity
    D. *improves* the soil's ability to absorb water
    E. *augments* soil fertility

40. *What* are the *common* symptoms of White Pine Blister Rust?   40. __
    A. Foliage turns yellow, then brownish
    B. Root collar and roots of seedlings rise above the sur-
       face of the soil
    C. Failure of seeds to germinate or seedlings to emerge
    D. Round or spindle-shaped swelling near the base of the stem
    E. Dead or partially killed seedlings with branch and stem
       swelling

41. All of the following are good understory soil-builders EXCEPT:41. __
    A. Redbud   B. Beech   C. Dogwood   D. Ash   E. Birch

42. *Which* of the following have *similar* results on the forest   42. __
    soil?
    I. Severe insect infestation   II. Clear-cutting
    III. Monoculture stands   IV. Grazing
    V. Prescribed burning

    The CORRECT answer is:
    A. I,IV,V   B. II,III,IV   C. II,IV,V
    D. All of the above   E. None of the above

6

43. About *what* percent of the total land area of the United   43. ___
    States is called "range" in reference to its use by livestock?
    A. 10%   B. 20%   C. 30%   D. 40%   E. 50%

44. *Which* of the following is NOT a way in which animals may   44. ___
    change the composition of vegetation? By
    A. trampling   B. disseminating seed
    C. contributing to soil fertility through animal waste
    D. eating forage
    E. grazing

45. *Which* of the following are TRUE?   45. ___
    I. Vegetation is intimately involved in the management of
       soil
   II. Grazing has a stimulating effect on growth
  III. Standards of range-use are based on plant indicators
   IV. There is no sharp line separating grazing lands that
       are classified as pasture from those classified as
       range
    V. Grazing is an essential agent in the building of soil

    The CORRECT answer is:
    A. I,III   B. II,IV,V   C. II,III,V   D. I,II,IV
    E. All of the above

46. All of the following accompany primary succession EXCEPT: 46. ___
    A. Build-up of mulch   B. Increase in soil structure
    C. Additional activity of micro-organisms
    D. More luxuriant plant growth
    E. Decrease in the amount of pore space

47. *How* is soil management accomplished on range areas? By   47. ___
    A. *administering* fertilizer
    B. *applying* agronomic principles
    C. *manipulating* grazing animals
    D. *protecting* the soil against water erosion
    E. *planting* herbaceous plants

48. All of the following are results of heavy grazing EXCEPT: 48. ___
    Heavy grazing
    A. *reduces* the growth of roots
    B. *produces* more pounds of beef per acre
    C. *results* in fewer seedstalks among forage species
    D. *affects* water absorption by decreasing the infiltration
       rate
    E. *decreases* forage production

49. Deferred and rotational grazing are very effective on _____   49. ___
    ranges.
    A. mesquite   B. bunchgrass   C. rabbitbrush
    D. goatweed   E. sagebrush

50. *What* do Nectria Canker, Beech Bark Disease, and Chestnut
Blight have in common? They are all
    A. non-infectious diseases caued by environmental conditions
    B. root diseases
    C. foliage diseases
    D. stem diseases
    E. systemic diseases of physiological origin

——————

KEY (CORRECT ANSWERS)

1.	C	11.	D	21.	A	31.	C	41.	
2.	D	12.	D	22.	E	32.	D	42.	
3.	E	13.	C	23.	C	33.	A	43.	
4.	D	14.	D	24.	B	34.	A	44.	
5.	E	15.	B	25.	A	35.	C	45.	
6.	E	16.	C	26.	B	36.	C	46.	
7.	A	17.	E	27.	B	37.	D	47.	
8.	B	18.	A	28.	C	38.	D	48.	
9.	A	19.	D	29.	B	39.	E	49.	
10.	C	20.	D	30.	B	40.	E	50.	

——————

EXAMINATION SECTION
TEST 1

Directions: Each question or incomplete statement is followed by several suggested answers or completions. Select the one that BEST answers the question or completes the statement. *PRINT THE LETTER OF THE CORRECT ANSWER IN THE SPACE AT THE RIGHT.*

1) _____ refers to a ranger's power or right to give commands, enforce obedience, take action and make decisions.

1. _____

   A.   Jurisdiction
   B.   License
   C.   Authority
   D.   Sanction

2) The primary objective of most of a park ranger's enforcement actions is

2. _____

   A.   correction and punishment
   B.   establishing authority and control
   C.   education and information
   D.   decreasing liability

3) Which of the following ranger services is LEAST likely to be provided through visitor contact?

3. _____

   A.   Interpretive
   B.   Resource management
   C.   Safety
   D.   Search, rescue and recovery

4) A ranger comes upon a location that she believes to be a crime scene, but she has no training in criminal investigation. As the first park official on the scene, she should

4. _____

   A.   disperse everyone in the area
   B.   record existing and relevant data in a notebook
   C.   straighten or clean up the scene
   D.   interview available witnesses

5) In most automobiles, the VIN plate is on the

5. _____

   A.   driver's side doorjamb
   B.   driver's side windshield post
   C.   driver's side dashboard
   D.   passenger's side dashboard

6)   A park's "situation map" should be marked on a surface of   6. _____

A.   wood or plywood
B.   paper
C.   enamel or clear acetate
D.   canvas

7)   The Rhomberg test is a field test most useful for indicating _____   7. _____
_____ intoxication.

A.   alcohol
B.   marijuana
C.   cocaine
D.   methamphetamine

8)   A ranger on patrol should imagine his/her key responsibility to be   8. _____

A.   conservation
B.   prevention
C.   surveillance
D.   observation

9)   The form of federal jurisdiction that a park ranger will encounter most   9. _____
rarely is _____ jurisdiction, which means the federal govern-
ment has been granted the right by a state to exercise certain state authorities.

A.   partial
B.   proprietary
C.   multiple
D.   concurrent

10)   One of the actions within a park ranger's continuum of enforcement   10. _____
levels is the verbal warning. The key to issuing a verbal warning is for a park
ranger to

A.   maintain a stern and authoritative tone of voice
B.   convince the offender of the seriousness of the offense
C.   convince the offender that the warning is really just a friendly chat
D.   be certain he has the authority to implement the consequences if it
becomes necessary

11) For most park agencies, the most appropriate training vehicle for providing training to rangers who will have law enforcement authority includes a

    11. _____

    I.   basic agency-wide course of 40 to 80 hours
    II.   20- to 40-hour orientation course at the assigned park
    III. 3- to 6-month on-the-job training program at the assigned park
    IV. participation in special training courses as opportunities arise.

A.   I and II
B.   II and III
C.   II, III and IV
D.   I, II, III and IV

12) Generally, the use of vehicles for park patrol

    12. _____

    I.   greatly increases a ranger's ability to respond quickly to emergencies
    II.   is the optimal method for increasing personal contact with visitors
    III. affords the ranger a degree of protection
    IV. offers the most efficient method of patrol with limited man power

A.   I, II and III
B.   I, III and IV
C.   II and III
D.   I, II, III and IV

13) Whenever a suitable wall surface isn't available for conducting a search of an offender, a kneeling search may be appropriate. In a standard kneeling search, the

    13. _____

A.   offender's knees should be together
B.   offender's feet should be spread apart
C.   offender's hand should be raised high above his head
D.   ranger should search from behind the offender

14) When initiating communication with visitors in an enforcement situation, the ranger's most immediate responsibility is to

    14. _____

A.   help the visitor understand the seriousness of the offense
B.   create a supportive rather than defensive climate
C.   make sure the visitor is aware of the ranger's authority to enforce
D.   ensure that the visitor is physically incapable of mounting an attack

15) Which of the following types of knots is used to attach a rope to the middle of another rope?

15. _____

A. Prusik
B. Clove hitch
C. Square lashing
D. Shear lashing

16) Listening is usually thought of as being accomplished on four levels. The highest level involves

16. _____

A. listening with understanding of the speaker's point of view
B. making sense out of sound
C. critically evaluating what is said
D. understanding the literal meaning of what is said

17) Which of the following structures may generally be entered unconditionally by a ranger in an enforcement situation?

17. _____

I. Park administrative building
II. Public restrooms
III. Visitor abodes
IV. Concessionaire's leased building

A. I and II
B. I, II and III
C. II and III
D. I, II, III and IV

18) Which of the following is most likely to be a standard item for a mounted patrol?

18. _____

A. Animal noose
B. Survival kit
C. Flares
D. Hydraulic jack

19) "Thumbnail" descriptions of persons include each of the following, EXCEPT

19. _____

A. Hair color
B. Eyes
C. Clothing
D. Race

20)   A ranger is reading a park map grid reference. On such maps, a four-digit grid reference number refers to the grid square located to the _____ _____ the point of intersection of the lines relating to the grid numbers.

20. _____

A.   right and above
B.   right and below
C.   left and above
D.   left and below

21)   It is usually permissible to search an offender incidental to an arrest. Which of the following statements about such searches is TRUE?

21. _____

A.   During a legal search, a ranger may seize items that are not only in actual possession, but within reach of the person at the time of the search.
B.   Evidence of a crime other than the one for which the ranger has an arrest warrant is generally not seizable .
C.   Stop-and-frisk searches are permitted under most situations.
D.   A legal search may usually be conducted by any ranger who has arrest powers.

22)   A ranger is helping to compose the interpretive text for visitor center exhibits. The best text-on-background color combination in terms of legibility would be

22. _____

A.   black on white
B.   green on white
C.   green on red
D.   blue on white

23)   Before conducting a search, a park ranger should always obtain a search warrant if there is time, or whenever there is doubt as to whether one is necessary. Generally, a search warrant is required if

23. _____

A.   exceptional circumstances create probable cause that contraband or other evidence will soon be destroyed
B.   the search is of a motor vehicle that is capable of being moved out of the ranger's control and there is probable cause to believe that someone in the vehicle has been involved in the commission of a crime
C.   the search is of a habitable dwelling on park grounds that is owned by the park, but occupied by the suspect as a camping abode
D.   the search is incidental to a lawful arrest and confined to the offender's person

24) A ranger should consider the primary objective of a park agency's interpretive services to be

24. _____

A. informing
B. dispelling commonly held assumptions
C. furthering an agenda
D. inciting the visitor to some action or feeling

25) In certain circumstances, search of a person or premises may be appropriate even though legal grounds are weak or absent. Such searches may be conducted with consent. Which of the following statements concerning consent searches is TRUE?

25. _____

A. The person granting consent does not necessarily have to be aware of the right to refuse consent.
B. A consent to enter premises implies a consent to search.
C. A statement welcoming a search implies that a warrant is not demanded.
D. Consent may be revoked at any time, but the revocation does not invalidate any evidence seized prior to the revocation.

KEY (CORRECT ANSWERS)

1. C
2. C
3. B
4. B
5. C

6. C
7. A
8. D
9. A
10. D

11. C
12. B
13. D
14. B
15. A

16. A
17. A
18. C
19. B
20. A

21. A
22. D
23. C
24. D
25. D

TEST 2

Directions: Each question or incomplete statement is followed by several suggested answers or completions. Select the one that BEST answers the question or completes the statement. *PRINT THE LETTER OF THE CORRECT ANSWER IN THE SPACE AT THE RIGHT.*

1) In most cases it is appropriate for a park ranger to think of visitors as

1. _____

    I.   not dependent on the ranger; it is the ranger who is dependent on them

    II.   the most important people the ranger will come into contact with

    III.   not an interruption of the ranger's work, but the main reason for it

    IV.   outsiders who will alter the park, rather than an integral part of the environment

A.   I and II
B.   I, II and III
C.   II, III and IV
D.   I, II, III and IV

2) Which of following legal terms is used to denote the proof that a crime has occurred?

2. _____

A.   *Corpus delicti*
B.   *Habeus corpus*
C.   *Respondeat superior*
D.   Probable cause

3) In the continuum of a park ranger's enforcement priorities, "Priority 1" situations deal with

3. _____

A.   the protection of visitors from each other
B.   situations in which neither the park nor its visitors are in any immediate danger
C.   the protection of the park's resources from the visitor
D.   the protection of visitors from hazardous conditions created by park resources

4)   The strongest ropes are generally made of   4. _____

A.   polypropylene
B.   nylon
C.   manila
D.   Dacron

5)   A ranger is helping to compose the interpretive text for visitor center   5. _____
exhibits. For one exhibit, visitors will be about 15 feet from the text. The letters for this text should be at least _____ high.

A.   a half-inch
B.   an inch
C.   an inch-and-a-half
D.   two inches

6)   The primary purposes of patrol include   6. _____

        I.   providing resource protection
        II.   making assistance available to visitors
        III.   providing a deterrent for destructive behavior
        IV.   observing the park and visitor behavior

A.   I and II
B.   II and IV
C.   II, III and IV
D.   I, II, III and IV

7)   A ranger is one of the first officials to arrive at the scene of a crime.   7. _____
Preliminary procedures that will ordinarily be undertaken by the investigating
ranger include each of the following, EXCEPT

A.   safeguarding the area
B.   conducting a methodic crime scene search
C.   separating witnesses from bystanders and obtaining statements
D.   rendering assistance to the injured

8)   In areas of _____ jurisdiction, only state law is considered   8. _____
to be in effect, meaning that federal officers may enforce rules and regulations
only such as Title 36, CFR and other federal laws allow regardless of jurisdiction.

A.   partial
B.   proprietary
C.   concurrent
D.   exclusive

9) To be legal, a search warrant should specifically identify the   9. _____

      I.   property to be seized
      II.   place to be searched
      III.   limits of the search
      IV.   probable cause upon which the search is based

A.   I and II
B.   II, III and IV
C.   III and IV
D.   I, II, III and IV

10) Which of the following is a guideline that should be followed in handling a domestic dispute on park property?   10. _____

A.   If the situation seems to justify the intervention of a professional counselor, recommend counseling in a general way.
B.   Offer legal advice if either of the parties is considering legal action.
C.   Ask questions that will determine who is at fault or who began the altercation.
D.   Try to stay out of such disputes unless it becomes clear that someone is in danger of imminent physical harm.

11) Rangers are often brought into contact with groups who represent "subcultures"—groups of a similar age, race, occupation or other grouping characteristics that may lead to the development of a kind of dialect or language system all their own. In communicating with these groups—especially in enforcement situations—it is important for the ranger to   11. _____

A.   acknowledge only standard grammatical English
B.   understand the "language" of the subculture, but not to use it
C.   try to communicate with these groups using their own dialect or jargon
D.   try to speak as little as possible

12) Rangers without law enforcement authority are empowered, in some situations, to   12. _____

      I.   issue citations
      II.   detain visitors
      III.   search visitors
      IV.   seize property

A.   I only
B.   I and II
C.   I, II and III
D.   I, II, III and IV

13) Which of the following is a disadvantage associated with foot patrol?   13. _____

A.   Ranger's presence is suggested, rather than seen or heard
B.   Restricted to extensive-use areas
C.   Direct contact with visitors is inhibited
D.   Limited ability to respond to situations outside the immediate area

14) Guidelines for search-and-rescue operations within a park include   14. _____

   I.   Radio-equipped searchers should be sent to danger or vantage
          points.
   II.   If dogs are used, they should be on a leash.
   III.   Searches should generally not be continued after dark unless a
          life-or-death situation exists.
   IV.   Each searcher should periodically call out the name(s) of the
          lost person(s).

A.   I and II
B.   I, II and III
C.   IV only
D.   I, II, III and IV

15) The ability of park rangers to implement enforcement services is de-   15. _____
pendent upon a number of factors. Which of the following is LEAST likely to
be one of these factors?

A.   The park agency's policies
B.   The ranger's level of certainty about the appropriateness of enforce-
ment
C.   The individual ranger's level of training and expertise
D.   The authority and jurisdiction authorized by law

16) Good listening skills for rangers include   16. _____

   I.   Forming judgements before listening to the speaker, based on
          appearance and demeanor
   II.   Considering listening to be an active process
   III.   Always taking notes while listening
   IV.   Listening to how something is being said before concentrating
          on the actual content of the message

A.   I and II
B.   II only
C.   II, III and IV
D.   I, II, III and IV

17)   Which of the following is NOT generally considered part of the standard frisk procedure?   17. _____

A.   Offender's feet spread about two feet apart.
B.   Offender's hands extended above the head, with fingers spread.
C.   Ranger moves fingertips over all searchable areas, crushing clothing to locate concealed weapons.
D.   Offenders considered dangerous should be handcuffed prior to the frisk.

18)   One of the signs that a person has overdosed on a stimulant is   18. _____

A.   cold, clammy skin
B.   fatigue
C.   slurred speech
D.   convulsions

19)   Which of the following is NOT a guideline that should usually be followed in conducting patrols?   19. _____

A.   Patrols should always follow the same method, route, and schedule.
B.   Patrol rangers should periodically stop at "overview" points.
C.   Open patrol is, in most situations, preferred to hidden patrol.
D.   Whenever possible, patrols should be conducted by a team of two.

20)   In relaying a description of an individual, the first detail given is usually   20. _____

A.   sex
B.   age
C.   race
D.   height

21)   Normally, searches of vehicles by a park ranger require a search warrant. Exceptions include   21. _____

    I.   whenever probable cause to search exists
    II.   the search is incidental to an arrest
    III.   items are in open view through the vehicle's window
    IV.   the vehicle has stopped at an authorized roadblock

A.   I only
B.   I and II
C.   I, II and III
D.   I, II, III and IV

22) Which of the following is LEAST likely to be a standard item for a   22. _____
cycle patrol?

A.   Portable spotlight
B.   First aid kit
C.   Maps and brochures
D.   Folding shovel

23) A ranger must attempt to stop a moving vehicle to implement an en-   23. _____
forcement action. While in motion, the ranger should stay within _____
_____ feet of the vehicle

A.   15 and 20
B.   25 and 40
C.   50 and 75
D.   100 and 200

24) Research demonstrates that _____ percent of a ranger's duty   24. _____
time involves some form of communication.

A.   55-65
B.   65-75
C.   75-85
D.   85-95

25) A ranger is called on to approach an offender who is belligerent.   25. _____
Guidelines to follow during such an encounter include

I.   making sure that a weapon is visible and at the ready
II.   trying to bargain with the offender for better behavior
III. if you do not have the authority to make an arrest, trying to
      give the impression that you do
IV.   regardless of the provocation, never exhibiting anger or impa
      tience

A.   I only
B.   I and II
C.   IV only
D.   II, III and IV

KEY (CORRECT ANSWERS)

1. B
2. A
3. A
4. B
5. B

6. D
7. B
8. B
9. D
10. A

11. B
12. A
13. D
14. D
15. B

16. B
17. C
18. D
19. A
20. A

21. C
22. D
23. C
24. C
25. C

TEST 3

Directions: Each question or incomplete statement is followed by several suggested answers or completions. Select the one that BEST answers the question or completes the statement. *PRINT THE LETTER OF THE CORRECT ANSWER IN THE SPACE AT THE RIGHT.*

1)   A ranger is composing a sketch of an accident scene. He will need to discriminate between temporary, short-lived, and long-lived evidence. Which of the following would be considered short-lived evidence?

   1. _____

A.   Gasoline puddles
B.   Vehicle debris
C.   Skid marks
D.   Gouges in the pavement

2)   In most situations, the best attitude for the park ranger to adopt is one that is _____-oriented.

   2. _____

A.   service
B.   enterprise
C.   task
D.   staff

3)   In the park setting, courts have ruled that search-and-seizure laws apply to visitor abodes (motor homes, trailers, screen canopies, rented cabins), as well as the area surrounding the abode and normally considered a part thereof (campsite, trash can, storage shed, etc.). The legal term for this surrounding area is

   3. _____

A.   environs
B.   curtilage
C.   quadrangle
D.   milieu

4)   Which of the following is NOT a guideline that a park ranger should use in handling a complaint?

   4. _____

A.   Remember that some complaints should be taken more seriously than others
B.   Focus initially on the facts surrounding the situation or problem
C.   Always thank the complainant for his or her interest
D.   Notify the complainant when corrective action has been taken

5) Guidelines for a park ranger's enforcement actions include 5. _____

    I.   the use of physical force should be limited to the minimum necessary to implement the action

    II.   the vigor or severity of enforcement actions should be dependent on the attitude of the offender

    III.   whenever a ranger is unable to secure cooperation, he should withdraw from the immediate area and seek appropriate assistance

    IV.   whenever doubt exists as to whether a situation actually constitutes a violation, or whether the suspect is in fact the perpetrator, the ranger should rule in favor of the visitor and try to resolve the doubt

A. I and II
B. I, III and IV
C. I and IV
D. I, II, III and IV

6) A park ranger should usually think of her primary duty as 6. _____

A. assuring each park visitor a quality experience
B. enforcing the existing rules within park boundaries
C. observing visitor behaviors and being prepared for any problems that might arise
D. protecting the park's most important resources

7) Which of the following is NOT a principle that should guide the composition and delivery of interpretive services in a park? 7. _____

A. Interpretation should tell the whole story, rather than just a part of it.
B. Interpretation should arouse curiosity in addition to giving facts.
C. The best interpretation sticks to information within the "comfort zone" of visitors.
D. The best interpretation occurs through person-to-person communication.

8) _____ patrol is the method that provides the greatest 8. _____
amount of visitor access, but usually prohibits extensive observation of visitor behavior and park conditions.

A. Cycle
B. Mounted
C. Foot
D. Vehicle

9)   One of the signs that a person has overdosed on a depressant is   9. _____

A.   hallucinations
B.   slow pulse
C.   cold, clammy skin
D.   constricted pupils

10)   A ranger is conducting a field interview to determine the cause of an   10. _____
incident. The ranger should know that of all the behaviors that suggest an
untruthful response, the one most commonly demonstrated by deceitful people
is

A.   bringing the hand to the head
B.   interrupting the questioner
C.   hesitation
D.   crossing the arms over the chest

11)   A ranger is conducting a field interview to record a visitor's percep-   11. _____
tions of an event. In recording the visitor's account, the ranger should remember each of the following general truths about human perception, EXCEPT
that

A.   people tend to overestimate the length of verticals while underestimat-
ing the width of horizontals
B.   danger and stress cause people to underestimate duration and distance
C.   light-colored objects tend to be seen as heavier and nearer than dark
objects of the same size and distance away
D.   people usually recall actions and events better than objects

12)   If a DWI suspect refuses to submit to a chemical test, many jurisdic-   12. _____
tions accept this as an admission of intoxication resulting in the revocation of
driving privileges for a period of time. This result, however, is predicated on
several criteria. Which of the following is NOT one of these criteria?

A.   The ranger has probable cause to believe the suspect is DWI.
B.   The suspect has already completed a standard field sobriety test.
C.   The ranger placed the suspect under arrest.
D.   The ranger specifically requested the suspect to submit to a chemical
test.

13)   A ranger is reading a park map grid reference. On this map, the num-   13. _____
bers are read from

A.   left to right and top to bottom
B.   left to right and bottom to top
C.   right to left and top to bottom
D.   right to left and bottom to top

14) Defensive measures consist of several levels of defense. The level known as "defensive opposition" involves

14. _____

A.   warding off blows with limbs or a baton
B.   the use of a firearm
C.   the use of chemical irritants
D.   simply ignoring verbal and visual abuse

15) Which of the following is NOT an element of the "legal scope" of a park ranger's jurisdiction?

15. _____

A.   The park's physical boundaries
B.   Traffic codes
C.   Fish and game laws
D.   Criminal statutes

16) Which of the following is an example of a "transitional" interpretive experience?

16. _____

A.   Slide presentation
B.   Visitor center exhibit
C.   Outdoor interpretive stations
D.   Automobile tour

17) A ranger is designing an interpretive activity for a group of elementary school children who are all about eight years old. For children at this age,

17. _____

A.   ideas, rather than objects, are very important
B.   relations with others are based primarily on self-interest
C.   there is a strong desire for independence from adults
D.   peer relationships are very important

18) Which of the following is most likely to be a standard item for a foot patrol?

18. _____

A.   Jumper cables
B.   Tranquilizer gun
C.   Folding stretcher
D.   Transceiver

19) In the continuum of a park ranger's enforcement priorities, "Priority 3" situations deal with   19. _____

A. the protection of visitors from hazardous conditions created by park resources
B. the protection of the park's resources from the visitor
C. the protection of visitors from each other
D. situations in which neither the park nor its visitors are in any immediate danger

20) Recreational resources may be managed under the guidance of several viewpoints. The _____ viewpoint holds that resources should be used in an essentially "as is" manner, and that visitor use should blend with the resource base.   20. _____

A. preservationist
B. landscape maintenance
C. conservationist
D. recreation activity

21) Which of the following is NOT a guideline that should be used for the conduct of station duty?   21. _____

A. Whenever rangers are in conversation with visitors, they should stand.
B. Each question should be answered as if it were the first time the ranger has heard it.
C. Rangers should remain sitting or standing behind a counter.
D. Rangers should attempt to serve all visitors who need assistance.

22) Which of the following statements about search warrants is typically FALSE?   22. _____

A. Searchers may remain only a sufficient length of time as is "reasonably" necessary to search for and seize the property described in the search warrant.
B. Generally, searchers may not seize items relating to criminal activity that are not specifically identified in the search warrant
C. Search warrants for the premises do not permit a search of all persons present in the premises
D. In most situations, real estate can be seized under a search warrant

23) A ranger's boundary maintenance responsibilities typically include each of the following functions, EXCEPT

23. _____

A. physically locating the boundary line, either by previous marks or survey
B. identifying trespass and/or encroachment
C. marking and signing the boundary
D. preventing erosion of coastal/shoreline boundaries

24) The park's public relations program must

24. _____

I. emphasize specific stages in a process, rather than ultimate goals
II. solve the problems of others while solving the problems of the park
II. focus on challenges and shortcomings that are in need of assistance or support
IV. consist of actions that are coordinated and integrated

A. I only
B. I, II and III
C. II and IV
D. I, II, III and IV

25) Arrests can normally be made by park rangers

25. _____

I. on an arrest warrant
II. on view of a felony being committed
III. on reasonable suspicion of a felony
IV. on reasonable suspicion of a misdemeanor

A. I only
B. I and II
C. I, II and III
D. I, II, III and IV

KEY (CORRECT ANSWERS)

1. C
2. A
3. B
4. A
5. B

6. A
7. C
8. C
9. C
10. A

11. B
12. B
13. B
14. A
15. A

16. D
17. D
18. D
19. B
20. C

21. C
22. D
23. D
24. C
25. C

EXAMINATION SECTION

DIRECTIONS: Each question or incomplete statement is followed by several suggested answers or completions. Select the one that BEST answers the question or completes the statement. *PRINT THE LETTER OF THE CORRECT ANSWER IN THE SPACE AT THE RIGHT.*

1. LEAST likely to affect specie habitation is
    A. geographic area
    B. quantity of vegetation
    C. human population
    D. diversity of vegetation
    E. types of nearby housing developments

1.____

2. Raccoons are *most likely* to be found in
    A. residential neighborhoods
    B. rural agricultural areas
    C. shores of coastal cities
    D. wooded suburbs
    E. reservoirs or other water bodies

2.____

3. A development well-endowed with wildlife benefits a developer by
    A. decreasing construction costs
    B. reducing erosion
    C. increasing property values
    D. reducing waste
    E. giving personal satisfaction

3.____

4. What do surveys of suburban and urban residents indicate about home owners' attitudes toward wildlife on their premises?
    A. Most homeowners appreciate the presence of wildlife
    B. Homeowners show no strong feeling toward the issue
    C. Homeowners appreciate wildlife in the area, but not on their premises
    D. Homeowners have a negative attitude toward wildlife
    E. Few homeowners appreciate wildlife on their premises

4.____

5. Pigeons and starlings are *less* popular than other birds because their droppings
    A. deface buildings
    B. cause deterioration of the water supply
    C. are a hazard to human health
    D. damage plants
    E. attract rodents

5.____

6. Of the following groups of wildlife, which are MOST affected by the use of pesticides in suburban homes and gardens?
    A. Birds   B. Mammals   C. Amphibians
    D. Reptiles   E. Fish and other aquatic animals

6.____

7. MOST likely to adapt to an almost complete loss of its salt marsh habitat is the
   A. fiddler crab   B. egret   C. mallard
   D. killifish   E. osprey

7. ____

8. What aspect of urbanization *particularly* affects marine species like the sea turtle?
   A. High noise levels   B. Bright city lights
   C. Large amount of refuse D. Presence of humans
   E. Use of pesticides

8. ____

9. The BEST way of avoiding conflict between urban wildlife and human residents is by
   A. correct planning to eliminate future problems
   B. education of residents
   C. elimination of wildlife
   D. development of problem solving devices
   E. reduction of wildlife

9. ____

10. Reflective glass should be used in
    A. buildings in wooded areas
    B. buildings near water
    C. areas where the buildings would normally attract nuisance birds
    D. all new urban buildings
    E. none of the above

10. ____

11. Of little concern to the urban wildlife planner is
    A. winter-feeding
    B. erection of artificial nesting structures
    C. habitat management
    D. artificial stocking
    E. transplanting of wildstock

11. ____

12. The conventional subdivision type of development allows
    A. more latitude in architectural design
    B. more planning opportunities for the community
    C. easy modification of lots
    D. more diverse movement corridors
    E. landscaping by individual lots

12. ____

13. Wildlife have a *greater* affinity to natural coniferous woodlands rather than coniferous plantations because
    A. plantations allow too much light to penetrate the woodland floor
    B. plantation trees are uniformly spaced
    C. the soils of plantations are too enriched
    D. plantations have little understory
    E. plantations lack woodland borders

13. ____

14. Similar woodlands located adjacent to dissimilar habitats would exhibit
    A. no differences
    B. imperceptible differences
    C. noticeable, but insignificant, differences
    D. significant differences
    E. one cannot tell from the information given

14. ____

15. The wildlife planner should locate food sources near   15.____
    A. nesting grounds   B. water
    C. cover   D. woodland edges
    E. residential properties

16. The types and populations of wildlife existing in an area   16.____
    can be determined by
    A. consulting trained biologists
    B. consulting regional and national species lists
    C. listing those species whose geographic range includes
       the proposed site
    D. listing *only* those species identified as common to the site
    E. conducting on-site inspections

17. Compensating for reducing the size requirements of wildlife17.____
    in the area can be made by
    A. increasing the amount of cover
    B. diversifying the space
    C. maintaining a wildlife corridor system
    D. providing a high quality habitat
    E. focusing attention on the requirements of the smaller
       species

18. Woodlands of GREATEST value to wildlife are   18.____
    A. coniferous   B. deciduous
    C. upland   D. semiwood floodplains
    E. wooded floodplains

19. The value of old fields is significantly INCREASED when   19.____
    they are adjacent to
    A. meadows   B. wooded areas   C. orchards
    D. farmland   E. developed areas

20. Nature trails should be elevated over wet areas *primarily* 20.____
    to
    A. keep children on the trail
    B. provide safe footing
    C. enable people to derive benefit from wildlife
    D. avoid disturbance of vegetation
    E. prevent access to wildlife

21. Pigeons and starlings successfully nest in urban areas   21.____
    because
    A. they do not need time to acclimate themselves to new
       conditions
    B. buildings provide nesting areas
    C. they are attracted to the small ornamental trees and
       fountains found in front of buildings
    D. they are unaffected by reflective glass
    E. their need for cover is minimal

22. Regional wildlife considerations focus *mainly* on   22.____
    A. artificial stocking   B. creation of refuges
    C. preservation   D. transplanting wildlife
    E. predator control

23. Maintenance of a wider diversity of wildlife species is   23.____
    possible on a *regional* basis because
       A. more money is available
       B. more flexibility is allowed
       C. large amounts of open space is provided
       D. individual residents are not involved
       E. plans are centralized

24. Which of the following contribute to making better use of 24.____
    urban open space?
        I. Closing off little used streets
       II. Using parallel rather than diagonal parking
      III. Turning alley junkyards into center block paths
       IV. Developing less intensive use of existing parks
        V. Rehabilitating empty lots
    The CORRECT answer is:
       A. I, II, III   B. II, III, IV   C. III, IV, V
       D. III, IV *only* E. I, III, V

25. During clean-up operations, which of the following should 25.____
    be removed?
       A. Dead and hollow trees   B. Trees with dead limbs
       C. Trees with dead tops   D. Fallen logs and sticks
       E. None of the above

26. The MOST likely reason why urban soils fail to continue to 26.____
    to support the growth of healthy trees is
       A. inadequate fertilization   B. salt content
       C. pedestrian traffic   D. nutrient depletion
       E. prior construction activity

27. Species typical of urban areas can survive WITHOUT   27.____
       A. cover   B. understory
       C. wide corridors   D. a home range
       E. all of the above

28. All of the following are examples of marsh and aquatic   28.____
    plants EXCEPT
       A. bullrush   B. smartweed   C. widgeon grass
       D. doveweed   E. spike rush

29. Many trees should be planted in natural situations in re-   29.____
    habilitation projects *primarily* to
       A. buffer human encroachment
       B. reduce the need for insecticides
       C. produce an aesthetically appealing landscape
       D. reduce maintenance costs
       E. reduce the threat of disease

30. Remedial measures are *usually* NOT effective in the case of 30.____
    streams
       A. degraded by siltation
       B. converted into enclosed storm sewers
       C. that have been channeled
       D. degraded by pollution
       E. all of the above

31. Better suited to cold water ponds are   31._____
    I. bluegills   II. lake trout
    III. catfish   IV. small mouth bass
    V. large mouth bass
    The CORRECT answer is:
    A. I, III *only*   B. II, IV *only*   C. I, III, V
    D. I, III, IV   E. I, II, III

32. Ponds classified as cold water ponds do NOT exceed tem-   32._____
    peratures of ____ degrees F.
    A. 50   B. 55   C. 60   D. 65   E. 70

33. Fish in a wildlife impoundment are denied access to nesting   33._____
    sites by
    A. lowering water levels   B. raising water levels
    C. installing deflectors   D. installing check dams
    E. encouraging the growth of aquatic vegetation

34. A pond deemed a safety hazard is developed with   34._____
    A. very sttep banks
    B. thin aquatic vegetation
    C. a maximum center depth of 6 feet
    D. a posted sign listing vital information
    E. gentle sloping bottom to the maximum depth required

35. Detention and sediment ponds should be removed   35._____
    A. after the final grading of the developed site
    B. after construction has been completed
    C. after the removal of all sediment
    D. before occupation of the site
    E. at no times

36. What food should be used to attract ducks and geese to   36._____
    wet pits or lakes?
    A. Oats and apple   B. Sorghum and millet
    C. Corn and green wheat   D. Rice
    E. Alfalfa and barley

37. Eutrophication of water results in   37._____
    A. *increase* in variety of plant life
    B. *decrease* biomass of the lake
    C. *increase* in the transparency of the water
    D. *decrease* in dissolved oxygen levels
    E. excessive algae and weed growth

38. All of the following will resist tree invasion for many   38._____
    years EXCEPT
    A. sedge   B. greenbriar   C. witch hazel
    D. huckleberry   E. gray dogwood

39. The ____ of trees saved is MOST important to wildlife.   39._____
    A. species   B. age   C. condition
    D. height   E. productivity

40. All of the following are wildlife consideration regarding   40.____
new airport sites EXCEPT:
    A. Soil type
    B. Drainage conditions
    C. Type of vegetation present
    D. Human disturbance
    E. Land uses in surrounding areas

41. The game manager should avoid the use of a single tree   41.____
species from a single source because of the
    A. possibility that a replacement may be difficult to find
    B. lack of aesthetic value
    C. danger of epidemic disease
    D. development of a monoculture
    E. possibility that the species may not enhance the site

42. The MOST certain way to keep land open is by   42.____
    A. zoning
    B. land development ordinances
    C. conservation easements
    D. public acquisition
    E. use of a severance tax

43. The woody plant of GREATEST value in the United States,   43.____
regardless of region, is the
    A. alder   B. mesquite   C. oak
    D. dogwood   E. pine

44. Which of the following is *most likely* to act as oases for   44.____
small birds during migration?
    A. School yards
    B. Suburban water-recharge basins
    C. Reservoirs
    D. Crevices of buildings
    E. Parks

45. The ecological stability of a residential development may   45.____
be MOST accurately measured by
    A. evidence of wildlife
    B. presence of wooded properties
    C. a wide variety of wildlife species
    D. presence of nests
    E. ground cover and water supply

46. The MAIN reason people are opposed to having wildlife   46.____
in their vicinity is the
    A. nuisance of wildlife
    B. unsanitary conditions caused by them
    C. deterioration of the water quality
    D. hazard to human health
    E. damage done to plants and property

47. Wildlife and its supporting habitat give GREATEST benefit   47.____
to
    A. homeowners
    B. hobbyists and recreational enthusiasts
    C. children
    D. researchers
    E. educators

48. The design of storm detention ponds should MINIMIZE   48._____
    I. growth of vegetation
    II. damage to property
    III. hazards to children
    IV. harm to the multiple uses the pond can be put
    V. problems of removal
The CORRECT answer is:
    A. I, II, V   B. II, III, IV   C. I, II, III, V
    D. I, II, III   E. I, II, III, IV, V

49. The features of a dump site that will attract the LARGEST   49._____
    number of gulls are
    I. large, flat surfaces   II. fresh water supply
    III. trees at the edge   IV. vegetation for cover
    V. an open area
The CORRECT answer is:
    A. I, II, III   B. II, III, IV   C. I, II, V
    D. I, II, IV   E. II, III, V

50. Basically the same for MOST wildlife species are the   50._____
    I. size of the home range
    II. configuration of the home range
    III. food requirements
    IV. cover requirements
    V. water requirements
The CORRECT answer is:
    A. I, III, V   B. I, II, V   C. III, IV, V
    D. V only   E. None of the above

KEY (CORRECT ANSWERS)

1. C	11. A	21. B	31. B	41. C
2. D	12. E	22. C	32. E	42. D
3. C	13. D	23. C	33. A	43. C
4. A	14. D	24. E	34. E	44. E
5. A	15. C	25. E	35. E	45. C
6. E	16. A	26. E	36. C	46. E
7. C	17. D	27. C	37. E	47. C
8. B	18. E	28. D	38. A	48. B
9. A	19. B	29. D	39. A	49. C
10. E	20. D	30. B	40. D	50. E

EXAMINATION SECTION

DIRECTIONS: Each question or incomplete statement is followed by several suggested answers or completions. Select the one that BEST answers the question or completes the statement. *PRINT THE LETTER OF THE CORRECT ANSWER IN THE SPACE AT THE RIGHT.*

1. The MOST common wild mammal in an urban area is the   1.___
    A. opossum   B. norway rat
    C. house mouse   D. squirrel
    E. rabbit

2. The CHIEF benefit of fish and wildlife in urban and   2.___
    suburban areas is
    A. hunting opportunities
    B. enjoyment of fishing
    C. opportunity for hiking and nature photography
    D. people's enjoyment in day-to-day living situations
    E. enjoyment of bird watching

3. The need for better planning and environmental management   3.___
    measures is MOST evident in
    A. increased interest in urban wildlife research
    B. the rapid increase in developed land
    C. the high level of environmental quality demanded by
       the public
    D. the decrease in farmland
    E. the growth of endangered species

4. The percent of the American public that accounts for the   4.___
    purchase of at LEAST sixty pounds of seed a year is
    approximately
    A. 2   B. 10   C. 20   D. 45   E. 60

5. Prices paid for new housing developments are *directly*   5.___
    related to
    A. the presence of wildlife in the area
    B. the educational benefits derived from wildlife in
       the area
    C. preservation of open space and natural setting
    D. positive attitude toward wildlife
    E. the variety of the wildlife present within the area

6. Which of the following bird populations are likely to   6.___
    increase after the development of a new town on the site
    of sparsely populated farmland area?
      I. Mockingbirds
     II. Chipping sparrows
    III. Red-winged blackbirds
     IV. Grasshopper sparrows
      V. Song sparrows

The CORRECT answer is:
A. I, II, V
B. I, III, IV
C. I, III, V
D. II, IV, V
E. II, V

7. When adequate vegetation is retained, ____ may continue to flourish in urban areas.
A. squirrels
B. raccoons
C. opossums
D. rabbits
E. all of the above

7.___

8. The GREATEST number of cases of rabies have occurred in
A. dogs
B. rabbits
C. squirrels
D. skunks
E. raccoons

8.___

9. A key requirement in meeting the needs of wildlife is providing a(n) ____ habitat(s).
A. number of
B. specific type of
C. large
D. diverse
E. enclosed

9.___

10. The planner should provide *preferred* food items in order to
A. control the wildlife population to certain species
B. ensure the health of the preferred species
C. prevent damage to homeowners' property
D. compensate for lack of vegetation
E. maximize the retention of desired species

10.___

11. The key to wildlife management is
A. space
B. vegetation
C. free water
D. soil
E. predator control

11.___

12. Procedures for integrating wildlife considerations into small site design are:
I. Identify habitats of threatened species
II. Identify food plants
III. Analyze adjacent land areas
IV. Develop continuous open space wildlife corridors
V. Identify limiting factors on the site
The CORRECT answer is:
A. I, II, IV
B. I, II, V
C. I, IV, V
D. II, III, V
E. II, IV, V

12.___

13. The amount of understory is *particularly* IMPORTANT for residential developments in order to
A. compensate for inadequate overstory
B. help buffer the disturbing effects of humans and their pets
C. prevent wildlife from entering roadways
D. prevent damage to resident's property
E. attract larger mammals to the area

13.___

14. Utilized as food by wildlife are
    A. twigs   B. seeds
    C. bark   D. roots
    E. all of the above

14.____

15. An adjacent ____ would BEST enlarge the home range of a development site.
    A. cemetery   B. school yard
    C. parking lot   D. farm
    E. vacant lot

15.____

16. What action should the planner take when a desired species, though present in the region, does NOT exist on the site in its undeveloped stage?
    A. Attempt artificial stocking
    B. Retain habitats for preferred species
    C. Identify limiting factors and eliminate them
    D. Increase the percent of undeveloped land
    E. Plan for free water on the site

16.____

17. Major wildlife corridor systems should be developed
    A. perpendicular to each other, meeting near the center of the site
    B. perpendicular to each other, meeting near the edge of the site
    C. parallel to each other at opposite ends of the site
    D. parallel to each other at the center of the site
    E. in circular configuration around the perimeter of the site

17.____

18. The major corridor should
    A. encircle the site
    B. connect with the largest undeveloped tract adjacent to the site
    C. link all the secondary and tertiary corridors
    D. bisect the site
    E. encourage the movement of wildlife into and through residential areas

18.____

19. To MINIMIZE *adverse* impact on wildlife,
    I. road segments should be aligned to buffer human disturbance
   II. road systems should be planned where the open space system is wide
  III. large wooded areas should be kept intact
   IV. roads should be designed to parallel major corridor systems
    V. fewer roads of wider width are preferable to more numerous, narrow roads
The CORRECT answer is:
    A. I, II, III   B. I, III
    C. I, III, V   D. I, IV
    E. II, III, IV

20.____

20. Recommended as a means to discourage the activities of children in areas of particular value to wildlife is to
   A. post signs
   B. plant thorny vegetation
   C. erect fences
   D. limit road access
   E. dig trenches

21. It is preferable to place parking lots between buildings of shopping malls and the open space system because
   A. the hours of activity are limited
   B. human activity is directed away from the open space
   C. wildlife is less sensitive to vehicles
   D. the fringe of parking lots are used infrequently
   E. noise and activity levels are fairly constant

22. In regional planning wildlife considerations focus *mainly* on
   A. artificial stocking   B. creations of refuges
   C. preservation   D. transplanting wildstock
   E. predator control

23. Dystrophic conditions in a lake result in all the following EXCEPT
   A. high biomass
   B. great variation in specie
   C. lowered available oxygen
   D. a decrease in photosynthetic organisms
   E. an increase in anaerobic decomposition

24. The MAIN limiting factor for wildlife in urban areas is
   A. dense population
   B. small amount of open space
   C. pollution
   D. noise levels
   E. traffic

25. Of the following, the one which would be MOST affected by the removal of rotting logs from the developed area is
   A. grasshoppers   B. mice
   C. salamanders   D. crows
   E. frogs

26. The MOST serious effect of construction activities on urban soil is
   A. topsoil is mixed with subsoil
   B. no consideration is given to beneficial wildlife
   C. construction materials make up various percentages of the soil
   D. the presence of sewage sludge
   E. the use of soil for drainage

27. The BEST security measure in downtown parks is
    A. lighted walkways
    B. elimination of understory
    C. post signs diagramming the park's walkways and exits
    D. to avoid placing walkways near dense shrub plantings
    E. to avoid narrow, twisting walkways

27.___

28. The preferable means of enhancing and maintaining natural diversity is
    A. use of imported plant species
    B. use of native plant species
    C. reducing understory in favor of overstory
    D. removing dead or hollow trees
    E. all of the above

28.___

29. The one MOST affected by controlling the water level in an impoundment is
    A. waterfowl
    B. reptiles and amphibians
    C. fish
    D. soil
    E. vegetation

29.___

30. The result of a properly designed impoundment is to
    A. increase habitat diversity
    B. provide recreational benefits
    C. provide aesthetic benefits
    D. increase real estate values

30.___

31. Fishponds are designed with steep banks to
    A. discourage the growth of aquatic vegetation
    B. reduce erosion
    C. attract a broad variety of wildlife
    D. prevent seepage
    E. discourage human interference

31.___

32. A channelized stream can be developed so that the hydrolic features resemble unchannelized streams by
    A. increasing aquatic vegetation
    B. reducing aquatic vegetation
    C. installing deflectors, and check dams
    D. installing storm detention basins
    E. grading the site prior to channelization

32.___

33. Which of the following are criteria for designing a multi-purpose pond?
    I. Pond margins have a 3:1 slope to a depth of 3 feet
    II. Dense vegetation around the margins
    III. Gentle slope before drop off to maximum depth
    IV. Flat area exposed
    V. Maximum depth at center is 6 feet
The CORRECT answer is:
    A. I, II   B. I, III
    C. I, III, IV   D. I, III, V
    E. all of the above

33.___

6

34. Dentention and sediment ponds should be retained after
    housing construction is completed to
    A. trap natural drainage
    B. provide a valuable wetland habitat
    C. minimize washouts
    D. lower the cost of construction
    E. none of the above

34.___

35. All of the following channel improvements eliminate
    important aquatic habitats EXCEPT
    A. deflectors and low dams
    B. excessive use of culverts
    C. realignment of the stream course
    D. dredging
    E. use of concrete channels

35.___

36. All of the following are useful in the control of erosion
    and sedimentation EXCEPT
    A. using soils suited for development
    B. allowing the natural flow of run-off
    C. leaving the soil bare for the shortest time possible
    D. detaining run-off on the site to trap sediment
    E. releasing run-off safely to downstream areas

36.___

37. Old fields that are dominated by brown sedge or bunchgrass
    can be improved by
    A. irrigation   B. disking
    C. fertilization   D. reseeding
    E. mowing

37.___

38. Streets and highways should be routed so they do not cross
    A. old fields   B. wetlands
    C. reservoirs   D. woodland
    E. woodland edges

38.___

39. Of the following, the one which is *most likely* to
    discourage wildlife from airports is
    A. providing buildings with overhanging roofs
    B. foundation plantings
    C. building structures with flat gravel roofs
    D. locating the airport on sandy land with good drainage
    E. increase the number of runway marker lights

39.___

40. The one of the following which is INCORRECT is that the
    planner
    A. should not disturb the natural aspects of the land
    B. should not use biological systems to assimilate and
       dispose of man's wastes
    C. must realize that the stability of the ecosystem is
       related to its diversity
    D. should not expect cooperation and support of the
       community
    E. should not consider wildlife as an option

40.___

41. The MAJOR infrastructure stimulant for urban growth is (are)
    A. railroads   B. waste water facilities
    C. highways   D. farm land
    E. strip mine areas

41.___

42. Of the following, the one which would be MOST affected by road construction and subsequent traffic is (are)
    A. a population denied access to its hibernating or breeding areas
    B. nocturnal species
    C. non-migratory populations
    D. aquatic organisms
    E. parasitic organisms

42.___

43. MOST wildlife species in the suburban area are able to meet their water requirements through
    A. precipitation   B. ingestion of food
    C. sprinklers   D. city water supplies
    E. free water

43.___

44. The MOST basic approach for encouraging wildlife populations is
    A. creation of refuges
    B. transplanting of wild stock
    C. habitat management
    D. protection through regulations
    E. predator control

44.___

45. An eastern area with spacious lawns and extensive landscaping is *likely* to attract
    A. house sparrows   B. chickadees
    C. cardinals   D. yellow-throated vireos
    E. wood thrushes

45.___

46. Wildlife species show the STRONGEST affinity for
    A. deciduous woodlands   B. old fields
    C. creeks   D. marshes
    E. woodland edges

46.___

47. The MOST important thing(s) the understory provides is(are)
    A. more moisture   B. limited light
    C. protection   D. food and water
    E. cover and food

47.___

48. The benefit that can be derived for species on the site from adjoining open space areas is
    A. increased range
    B. refuge area
    C. diversified food supply
    D. sites for artificial nesting structures
    E. predator control

48.___

49. The one of the following which is MOST difficult to determine is (are)
    A. the type of wildlife existing in the area
    B. limiting factors for the preferred species
    C. habitats on the site
    D. the best use of adjacent open space
    E. the amount of open space required

49. ___

50. Which of the following are TRUE of planning corridor systems?
    I. All corridors do not have to be equal in length
    II. The major corridor should connect with the largest undeveloped tracts of land adjacent to the site
    III. Shrubbery should take precedence over trees
    IV. All corridors should be defined at the early planning stages
    V. As many corridors as possible should be planned
The CORRECT answer is:
    A. I, II, V
    B. I, II, IV, V
    C. I, III, IV
    D. II, IV, V
    E. all of the above

50. ___

KEY (CORRECT ANSWERS)

1. D	11. B	21. D	31. A	41. B
2. D	12. D	22. C	32. C	42. A
3. B	13. B	23. A	33. B	43. E
4. C	14. E	24. B	34. B	44. C
5. C	15. A	25. C	35. A	45. C
6. A	16. C	26. C	36. B	46. A
7. E	17. A	27. D	37. B	47. E
8. D	18. B	28. B	38. B	48. B
9. D	19. B	29. E	39. D	49. E
10. E	20. B	30. E	40. B	50. A

EXAMINATION SECTION

DIRECTIONS: Each question or incomplete statement is followed by several suggested answers or completions. Select the one that BEST answers the question or completes the statement. *PRINT THE LETTER OF THE CORRECT ANSWER IN THE SPACE AT THE RIGHT.*

1. Of the following, which would account MOST for the presence of birds in urban areas?   1.___
   A. Reservoirs   B. Dumps
   C. Tall buildings   D. Zoos
   E. Mast trees

2. Urbanization has helped to increase populations of amphibians and reptiles by   2.___
     I. providing ground cover
    II. eliminating natural predators
   III. creating breeding sites
    IV. draining wetlands
     V. providing a diverse habitat
   The CORRECT answer is:
   A. I, II   B. II, III
   C. II, IV, V   D. all of the above
   E. none of the above

3. The high urban squirrel populations can be accounted for by   3.___
   A. large, uncrowded and productive mast trees
   B. conifers
   C. reservoirs
   D. refuse dumps
   E. few predators

4. Most of the money spent on the enjoyment of nongame birds was spent on   4.___
     I. birdseed
    II. birdbaths
   III. books on birds
    IV. binoculars
     V. camera equipment
   The CORRECT answer is:
   A. I, II, III   B. I, II, III, IV
   C. I, III   D. I, III, IV
   E. I, IV, V

5. Trees enhance the value of property by *approximately* ____ percent.   5.___
   A. 2   B. 5   C. 10   D. 20   E. 30

6. The increase in mockingbirds in new town developments can   6.___
   be accounted for by an increase in
       A. coniferous woodland
       B. deciduous woodland
       C. the fruit bearing shrubs
       D. watercourses
       E. decorative landscaping

7. Man's PRINCIPAL impact on wildlife has been to alter the   7.___
   environment through
       A. hunting and fishing
       B. highway construction
       C. use of pesticides and fertilizers
       D. urbanization
       E. applied ecology

8. The GREATEST health hazard associated with gray squirrels   8.___
   is the
       A. transmission of rabies
       B. risk of infection from bites
       C. transmission of leptospirosis
       D. transmission of cryptococcosis
       E. spread of encephalitis from fleas

9. The area necessary to satisfy all of an animal's require-   9.___
   ments is called its
       A. territory   B. space
       C. home range   D. biosphere
       E. ecosystem

10. Wildlife management is defined as   10.___
       A. the act of producing sustained annual crops of wildlife
          to achieve human goals
       B. the conservation of endangered species
       C. the act of creating environmental enhancement
       D. the preservation of wanted species and the elimination
          of unwanted ones
       E. the act of sustaining wildlife for environmental,
          recreational and scientific values

11. The house sparrow would be the dominant nesting bird in an   11.___
    eastern metropolis with
       A. little or no empty space and few grassy areas or shrubs
       B. pleasant lawns of some size and a sprinkling of shrubs
       C. spacious lawns and extensive landscaping
       D. grassy lawns and shade trees
       E. older trees, many shrubs with mulch around them

12. The FIRST step in wildlife planning of a Planned Unit   12.___
    Development is to
       A. identify regional species that could be present with
          the proper habitat
       B. determine the amount of open space necessary
       C. identify habitats and their relative value
       D. identify limiting factors for preferred species
       E. identify food plants important to wildlife

13. When two deciduous habitats are similar, the one which
    should be chosen for site development is the one
       A. whose soil has a high moisture content
       B. requiring minimum maintenance
       C. with the denser understory
       D. with the greater overstory
       E. with less ground cover
13.___

14. The potential wildlife amenities within the proposed
    development and in adjacent residential areas will be
    MOST enhanced by
       A. limiting traffic to two lane roads
       B. providing movement corridors
       C. increasing acreage
       D. thinning the overstory canopy
       E. providing woodland edges
14.___

15. A linear configuration of the wooden tracts found in
    residential areas is suitable to songbirds because
       A. food is readily available
       B. it provides much edge
       C. it provides a buffer from the human population
       D. these birds are nonmigratory
       E. good moisture content of the soil is retained
15.___

16. The integration of wildlife habitats into the open space
    design begins in those areas
       A. best suited to desired wildlife
       B. with free water
       C. adjacent to open space areas
       D. that would be retained irrespective of wildlife
       E. preferable for use as recreational areas
16.___

17. The species which finds value in tertiary corridors con-
    sisting of rows of trees or shrubs along a road right-of-
    way is
       A. squirrels   B. raccoons
       C. garter snakes   D. rabbits
       E. none of the above
17.___

18. With respect to vehicles, MOST species will run when
       A. the vehicle is moving
       B. the engine is running
       C. the engine is shut off
       D. passengers stare out the windows
       E. headlights are turned off
18.___

19. A commercial development may help buffer the larger refuge
    components of the open space system because
       A. the activity does not affect adjacent open space areas
       B. the activity is continuous
       C. the grounds are landscaped
       D. activity is low or nonexistent in evenings and over
          weekends
       E. none of the above
19.___

20. The ability of nuisance birds to use urban buildings for
nesting is *most* attributed to the ____ of the buildings.
    I. design
   II. location
  III. exposure
   IV. construction
    V. height
The CORRECT answer is:
   A. I, II, III   B. I, II, V
   C. I, III   D. I, IV
   E. none of the above

20. ___

21. Regional planners can MAXIMIZE diversity of habitats by
   A. preserving limited and unique habitat types
   B. creating refuges
   C. maintaining the soil fertility and avoiding erosion
   D. managing existing vegetation and added plantings
   E. modifying sensitive areas

21. ___

22. The corridor system of larger-scale planning should be
based on
   A. floodplains present   B. wooded areas
   C. waterways   D. meadowlands present
   E. all of the above

22. ___

23. Landscaping in urban areas should be directed toward
selecting plant species that fit well into the urban environ-
ment and
   A. provide cover
   B. are aesthetically pleasing
   C. have food value for wildlife
   D. do not require much care
   E. are desirable for erosion control

23. ___

24. Which of the following are ways of protecting trees in
northern cities where deicing salts are used in large
quantities?
    I. Erecting snow fences
   II. Locating trees a distance from the road
  III. Improving road drainage systems
   IV. Treating root systems before planting
    V. Mixing salt with sand
The CORRECT answer is:
   A. I, II, III   B. I, III, IV
   C. I, IV, V   D. II, III, IV
   E. II, IV, V

24. ___

25. The SIMPLEST and MOST cost efficient method of recondi-
tioning urban soil is
   A. mixing topsoil with subsoil
   B. adding sewage sludge
   C. adding topsoil
   D. aeration
   E. use of fertilizers and insecticides

25. ___

26. Sensitive planting and design are CRITICAL in urban
    redevelopment projects because
    A. of the presence of dense population
    B. many buildings have reflective glass
    C. people are not accustomed to the needs of wildlife
    D. soils are usually poor
    E. undisturbed land and water is limited

    26.____

27. Most urban parks LACK
    A. native plant species   B. free water
    C. overstory   D. understory
    E. wild seeds

    27.____

28. The main reason that roads should be located far from
    streams is
    A. to discourage recreation activities
    B. accelerated erosion
    C. wildlife mortality
    D. noise levels
    E. pollution

    28.____

29. Watersheds filter strips bordering tributaries should be
    increased ____ feet for each one percent of slope.
    A. 1   B. 2   C. 4   D. 10   E. 12

    29.____

30. A depth of ____ feet around the margin of a pond dis-
    courages plant growth.
    A. 2   B. 3   C. 4   D. 5   E. 6

    30.____

31. Which of the following is MOST desirable for both fish
    and wildlife management purposes of a wildlife impoundment?
    A. A control structure to prevent changing temperatures
    B. A control structure to permit changing water levels
    C. Seasonal vegetation
    D. Shallow margins
    E. Steep margins

    31.____

32. Storm detention ponds and catchment basins should be
    installed
    A. prior to the initial grading of the development site
    B. after grading of the development site is completed
    C. during construction of the development site
    D. after construction of the development site
    E. at any time

    32.____

33. Water control structures and emergency spillways should be
    designed as permanent structures of storm detention ponds
    to
    A. minimize possible washouts
    B. meet safety requirements
    C. ensure sediment is trapped
    D. allow for the easy removal of sediment
    E. ensure the preservation of the pond

    33.____

34. What effect do the organic compounds in the effluent of   34.___
    septic tanks have on the receiving body of water?
    A. Available nitrates are decreased.
    B. CO_2 levels decrease.
    C. The pH of the water increase.
    D. The amount of dissolved oxygen is decreased.
    E. The basic oxygen demand of the water body decreases.

35. The BEST approach to managing existing open space areas is   35.___
    A. frequent mowing
    B. frequent fertilization
    C. periodic reseeding
    D. spraying with herbicides
    E. less frequent mowing

36. Food plots in old fields should be planted   36.___
    A. midway between travel corridors
    B. at a central location
    C. under overstory
    D. adjacent to good cover
    E. at locations that will equally distribute wildlife
       over the site

37. The MOST effective way of lowering highway deaths of deer   37.___
    is the use of
    A. tunnels underneath the highway
    B. deer-proof fences
    C. trenches
    D. natural vegetation
    E. warning signs for drivers

38. Which of the following will NOT reduce the bird hazard at   38.___
    airport sites?
    A. Retaining the squirrel population
    B. Keeping infield grass areas free of weeds
    C. Keeping infield grass areas at a height of 5-8"
    D. Prohibiting the growing of corn and sunflowers near
       the site
    E. Locating the dump on the same side as bodies of water

39. The Conservation Directory is of much use to the planner   39.___
    because it
    A. contains programs related to plant and animal species
    B. provides information on services rendered by federal
       departments
    C. provides information on wildlife planning and manage-
       ment
    D. lists organizations concerned with conservation programs
    E. lists wildlife and their habitats

40. The cultivated plant that is of the GREATEST value through-   40.___
    out the United States is
    A. corn   B. apple
    C. rice   D. cultivated cherry
    E. timothy

41. One effect of conventional residential developments is
    that
    A. smaller natural drainage channels are obliterated
    B. little space is left for natural vegetation
    C. bright lights confuse species' biorhythms
    D. erosion occurs
    E. the number of enclosed storm sewers decrease

41.___

42. ____ corridor(s) can be defined at the early planning
    stages.
    A. Primary   B. Secondary
    C. Tertiary   D. Ancillary
    E. none of the above

42.___

43. The people who tend to make the LEAST use of adjacent
    natural open space are those in
    A. townhouses
    B. low bedroom-count units
    C. high bedroom-count units
    D. garden apartments
    E. high rise apartments

43.___

44. The LEAST desirable area to locate a playground is near
    A. the edge of woodland areas
    B. orchards
    C. larger wooded areas
    D. old fields
    E. open areas with little vegetation

44.___

45. The MAJOR function of large-scale planning is to
    A. safeguard nesting sites
    B. establish wildlife inventories
    C. achieve aesthetic and environmental enhancement
    D. identify key wildlife areas that should be free from
       development
    E. review the site development plans of all developers

45.___

46. The BEST way for regional planners to identify the
    presence of endangered plant and animal species is by
    A. wildlife inventories
    B. local conservation groups
    C. state museum
    D. field surveys
    E. fish and game departments

46.___

47. The MOST common type of regulatory mechanism to preserve
    open space is
    A. zoning
    B. requiring an Environmental Impact Statement
    C. state law
    D. federal law
    E. individual policing and increasing awareness through
       education

47.___

48. Accumulation of excess salt in the root zones of urban trees can be prevented by
    A. digging a shallow trench around the tree
    B. fencing the planting area
    C. mounding the planting area
    D. flushing with water
    E. mulch around planting areas

48.___

49. If reflective glass is used on buildings, it should NOT reflect
    A. other buildings   B. the sky
    C. water   D. vegetation
    E. lights

49.___

50. Which of the following represents the BEST connecting links to planned urban open space?
    I. Nearby residential areas with small adjoining backyards
    II. Parkway right-of-way
    III. Parking lots
    IV. Railroad right-of-way
    V. Alley junkyards
    The CORRECT answer is:
    A. I, II, IV   B. I, III, V
    C. II, III, IV   D. II, IV, V
    E. III, V

50.___

KEY (CORRECT ANSWERS)

1. A	11. A	21. A	31. B	41. A
2. B	12. C	22. A	32. A	42. A
3. A	13. C	23. C	33. E	43. E
4. E	14. B	24. A	34. D	44. C
5. D	15. B	25. B	35. E	45. D
6. C	16. D	26. E	36. D	46. D
7. D	17. A	27. E	37. B	47. A
8. C	18. C	28. B	38. E	48. C
9. C	19. A	29. C	39. D	49. D
10. A	20. D	30. B	40. A	50. A

EXAMINATION SECTION

DIRECTIONS: Each question or incomplete statement is followed by several suggested answers or completions. Select the one that BEST answers the question or completes the statement. *PRINT THE LETTER OF THE CORRECT ANSWER IN THE SPACE AT THE RIGHT.*

1. ____ squirrels are found in northern urban areas where   1.___
    conifers predominate.
       A. Tree   B. Red
       C. Fox   D. Gray
       E. Flying

2. People prefer to live in communities in which wildlife   2.___
    has been integrated because of
       A. personal satisfaction
       B. ecological benefits
       C. environmental concerns
       D. the reduction of the insect population
       E. recreational benefits

3. Surveys indicate that the type of wildlife MOST desired   3.___
    by residents is
       A. squirrels   B. birds
       C. chipmunks   D. rabbits
       E. fish

4. The GREATEST impact on wildlife has been made by   4.___
       A. shooting and trapping of wildlife species
       B. alteration of the habitat
       C. waste disposal and pollution
       D. pesticides
       E. increased human population

5. The house sparrow population INCREASES after a new develop-   5.___
    ment replaces farmland because of
       A. an increase in nesting and roosting sites
       B. birdseed put out by residents
       C. the presence of deciduous trees
       D. the presence of fruit bearing shrubs
       E. an increase in insect population

6. Modification of aquatic habitats by drainage, dredging,   6.___
    pollution and removal of vegetation has serious effects on
    all amphibians EXCEPT those
       A. who are adapted to salt water
       B. whose egg and larvae stages are spent on land
       C. which are carnivorous
       D. which have internal development of eggs
       E. with dry, scaly skin

7. Animal control specialists have found that residents   7.___
    reporting damage by wildlife want
        A. advice on how to deal with the nuisance
        B. the animal killed
        C. the animal removed
        D. preserves set up by the authority
        E. wildlife departments to exert more control over
           wildlife

8. The amount and diversity of wildlife in urban and subur-   8.___
    ban areas is LIMITED by
        A. poor spatial configuration
        B. lack of connective open space
        C. failure to provide a specific type of habitat
        D. lack of small, disconnected woodlots
        E. all of the above

9. Which of the following poses the BIGGEST threat to wildlife? 9.___
        A. Free roaming cats and dogs
        B. Domestic livestock
        C. Children
        D. Indiscriminate use of poisons
        E. Presence of omnivorous opossums and raccoons

10. The planned unit development INCREASES the potential for   10.___
    wildlife amenities within the community because
        A. of the smaller human population
        B. unique habitat types can be preserved
        C. of the involvement of municipal and county planning
           departments
        D. there is more open space
        E. of better watershed planning

11. Habitat types for site planning can be identified by   11.___
    means of
        A. aerial photographs   B. vegetation maps
        C. water tables   D. field guides
        E. geographic guides

12. The habitat type that is LEAST attractive to wildlife is   12.___
        A. orchards   B. meadows
        C. old fields   D. farmland
        E. woodland edges

13. The purpose of tying a development to adjacent open space   13.___
    areas is that
        A. populations of wildlife are increased
        B. habitats can be improved
        C. movement corridors are unnecessary
        D. species requiring larger home ranges can be accommodated
        E. species can be isolated from human population

14. The planner can retain species sensitive to human dis-   14.___
    turbance by
        A. maintaining wooded tracts
        B. providing a high quality habitat
        C. providing acreage greater than that required under
           normal conditions
        D. providing food close to human occupied areas
        E. providing food far from human occupied areas

15. The MAIN purpose of developing corridor systems that meet   15.___
    near the center of the site is
        A. wider corridors are possible
        B. wildlife amenities are more concentrated
        C. less light penetration
        D. protection from human population
        E. equitable distribution of wildlife amenities

16. Evergreen shrubs are preferable for supplemental planting   16.___
    because they
        I. provide cover and screening all year
       II. are more resistant to disease
      III. are less conducive to erosion
       IV. reduce noise levels
        V. attract insects
    The CORRECT answer is:
        A. I, II, III   B. I, II, V
        C. I, III   D. I, IV
        E. I, V

17. _____ noise and movement have had the least effect on most   17.___
    species.
        A. Discontinuous   B. Intermittent
        C. Continuous   D. Sudden
        E. Furtive

18. To MINIMIZE the effects on wildlife, parking areas for   18.___
    small commercial facilities should be
        A. at the rear of the buildings
        B. in the front of the buildings
        C. evenly distributed around the building
        D. placed as buffers for the open space
        E. restricted to roadways

19. Runoff from agricultural land will have its GREATEST   19.___
    genetic effect on
        A. filter feeders
        B. photosynthetic organisms
        C. primary consumers
        D. bacteria
        E. predatory animals at the top of the food chain

20. MOST useful in evaluating wildlife habitats for large scale planning are
    A. aerial photographs
    B. vegetation maps
    C. wildlife inventories
    D. field surveys
    E. fish and game departments

20.___

21. Efforts on the regional level should be directed toward MAXIMIZING retention of large areas interconnected by smaller corridors to
    A. protect species from natural predators
    B. protect species from human intervention
    C. better distribute wildlife
    D. ensure retention of most species in the region
    E. accommodate species with large home range requirements

21.___

22. Plant selection in urban areas should attract
    A. squirrels   B. songbirds
    C. insects   D. house sparrows
    E. all of the above

22.___

23. The landscape design that would attract songbirds is
    A. tall trees with woodchip understory
    B. tall trees with shrub understory
    C. shrubs and small trees
    D. tall trees with nesting hollows
    E. small trees with grassy areas

23.___

24. The FIRST consideration in any urban redevelopment project is
    A. the relationship of planned open space to the surrounding area
    B. the width of the corridors
    C. the presence of stress factors
    D. public access
    E. the home range of the desired species

24.___

25. Great care is needed in selecting, planting and caring for trees and shrubs in urban areas due to
    A. the limited home range of the city environment
    B. poor soils, pollution and heavy usage
    C. the scarcity of wide corridors
    D. vandalism
    E. heavy use of insecticides

25.___

26. Natural meadows can be provided in urban parks by reducing the frequency of mowing to
    A. once in early spring
    B. once in late summer
    C. once in early spring and once in early fall
    D. three or four times a year
    E. once in mid summer

26.___

27. The LEAST benefit derived from buffer strips along
    streams is the
    A. prevention of erosion
    B. preservation of the stream channel's integrity
    C. prevention of storm damage
    D. maintenance of suitable water temperature
    E. provision of food

27.___

28. In a cold-water pond, the temperature is measured
     I. 6" below the surface
    II. during summer
   III. after sunset
    IV. during the early spring
     V. before sunrise
    The CORRECT answer is:
    A. I, II, III   B. I, II, V
    C. I, III   D. I, III, IV
    E. I, IV, V

28.___

29. Impoundments designed to attract a broad variety of
    wildlife should
    A. be shallow
    B. have a high water level
    C. have diversified margins
    D. have gentle sloping margins
    E. have steep margins

29.___

30. Wading birds or shorebirds will be attracted to areas
    A. of mud, silt, and shallow water
    B. dense vegetation
    C. thin vegetation
    D. where water temperatures fluctuate the least
    E. of stormwater detention basins

30.___

31. Which of the following design features are *recommended*
    for the safety of children playing in the area of a wild-
    life impoundment?
     I. Well vegetated
    II. Thinly vegetated
   III. Gently sloping banks
    IV. Shallow margins
     V. Steep margins
    The CORRECT answer is:
    A. I, III, IV   B. I, III, V
    C. I, IV   D. II, III, IV
    E. II, III, V

31.___

32. Sand, gravel pit, and stone quarries may be used for all
    the following EXCEPT
    A. flood-water storage
    B. desilting basins
    C. recreation lakes
    D. desalinization recharge basins
    E. fish and wildlife enhancement

32.___

33. Which of the following will help *reduce* shock loads on   33.___
    waters receiving runoff from urban roadways?
      I. Intensifying street cleaning operations
     II. Utilizing low curbs where the road is adjacent to
         grass areas
    III. Using nonporous pavement
     IV. Selecting roadway sites less likely to drain directly
         into the receiving body of water
      V. Detaining storm runoff
    The CORRECT answer is:
      A. I, II, IV   B. I, III, IV
      C. I, IV   D. I, IV, V
      E. all of the above

34. After a few years of cessation of mowing, there will be   34.___
    a(n)
      A. decrease in variation of plant life
      B. reduction of nitrate levels in the soil
      C. growth of woody vegetation
      D. increase in the erosion of soil
      E. decrease in the number of habitats

35. For both nesting and escape cover, MOST songbirds require   35.___
    ____ height and ____ cover.
      A. medium, dense   B. low, dense
      C. low, sparse   D. high, sparse
      E. high, dense

36. Which of the following should be planned to be UNATTRAC-   36.___
    TIVE to wildlife?
      A. Cemeteries   B. Golf courses
      C. Airports   D. Highways
      E. School grounds

37. The type of habitat that should be AVOIDED in managing   37.___
    metropolitan watersheds for water supply is
      A. deciduous woodland plantations
      B. living fences of shrubs
      C. bush and tree fruits
      D. orchards
      E. dense pine plantations

38. The planner can have soil testing done at the   38.___
      A. U.S. Department of the Interior
      B. U.S. Soil Conservation Service
      C. U.S. Geological Survey Center
      D. U.S. Department of Agriculture
      E. U.S. Agricultural Extension Service

39. The marsh and aquatic plant that is of the GREATEST   39.___
    value throughout the United States is
      A. water lily   B. cattail
      C. bristle grass   D. ragweed
      E. pondweed

40. Park maintenance should control woody vegetation
    A. before the nesting season
    B. at the beginning of the nesting season
    C. at the peak of the nesting season
    D. after the peak of the nesting season
    E. at any time

40.___

41. Watersheds filter strips bordering tributaries in flat
    terrain should be ____ feet wide.
    A. 10   B. 25   C. 50   D. 75   E. 100

41.___

42. Which of the following are better suited to a *warm* water
    pond?
      I. Large mouth bass
     II. Bluegills
    III. Catfish
     IV. Salmon
      V. Greyling
    The CORRECT answer is:
    A. I, II, III   B. I, III
    C. I, III, V   D. I, IV, V
    E. II, III, V

42.___

43. The productivity of a pond would be affected by
    A. siltation   B. evaporation
    C. oxygen content   D. nutrient content
    E. all of the above

43.___

44. The fish population of the wildlife impoundment can BEST
    be controlled by
    A. reducing the home range
    B. constructing islands
    C. attracting natural predators
    D. allowing recreational fishing
    E. restricting access to nesting sites

44.___

45. The MINIMUM depth of a pond located in cold climates that
    will prevent fish kill is ____ feet.
    A. 3   B. 6   C. 10   D. 15   E. 25

45.___

46. Storm detention ponds should be installed PRIOR to the
    grading of a development to
    A. ensure a wetland habitat to the site
    B. prevent spillways
    C. minimize erosion
    D. trap sediment generated by construction
    E. satisfy safety requirements

46.___

47. The bird that would show the MOST striking increase after
    a development replaces farmland is the
    A. mockingbird   B. mourning dove
    C. bobtail quail   D. starling
    E. song sparrow

47.___

48. What adverse effect do grey squirrels have on urban and suburban residents?   48. ___
    A. They transmit disease.
    B. Their droppings are unsanitary.
    C. They inflict serious wounds, particularly on children.
    D. They attract parasites.
    E. They damage buildings and property.

49. On institutional grounds, shrubbery should be placed   49. ___
    A. in clumps away from the buildings
    B. in clumps near or against the buildings
    C. in clean lines against the buildings
    D. in clean lines around borders
    E. singly and scattered

50. Which of the following has done the MOST to ensure wild-   50. ___
    life considerations on a project-by-project basis?
    A. Environmental impact statement requirements
    B. Land development ordinances
    C. The U.S. Environmental Protection Agency
    D. Conservation easements
    E. Use of severance tax

KEY (CORRECT ANSWERS)

1. B	11. B	21. D	31. A	41. C
2. E	12. A	22. B	32. D	42. A
3. B	13. D	23. B	33. D	43. E
4. B	14. C	24. A	34. C	44. E
5. A	15. E	25. B	35. A	45. D
6. B	16. D	26. B	36. C	46. D
7. A	17. C	27. C	37. E	47. D
8. B	18. B	28. B	38. E	48. E
9. A	19. E	29. D	39. E	49. A
10. D	20. D	30. A	40. D	50. A

EXAMINATION SECTION

DIRECTIONS: Each question or incomplete statement is followed by
several suggested answers or completions. Select the
one that BEST answers the question or completes the
statement. *PRINT THE LETTER OF THE CORRECT ANSWER
IN THE SPACE AT THE RIGHT.*

1. *Which* of the following are the *most important* hickories for   1. ___
mass production?
   I. Shagbark   II. Mockernut   III. Butternut
   IV. Sweetnut   V. Red Nut

   The CORRECT answer is:
   A. I,IV   B. I,II,IV   C. I,II,III   D. I,IV,V
   E. II,III,IV,V

2. *What* are some of the uses for prescribed burning? It is used 2. ___
   I. as the first step in seedbed preparation
   II. to stimulate regeneration of sprouts and seedlings
   III. to create openings in dense stands of brush
   IV. to produce a slight soil sterilant effect
   V. when only crown control is required

   The CORRECT answer is:
   A. III,IV,V   B. III,IV   C. I,II,III   D. II,V
   E. All of the above

3. *Which* of the following are *most important* in determining the 3. ___
method of seed storage?
   I. Seed characteristics   II. Time of storage
   III. Length of storage   IV. Seed quantity
   V. Climate

   The CORRECT answer is:
   A. I,II,V   B. I,III   C. II,III,V   D. I,III,IV
   E. II,III,IV,V

4. Seeds with impervious coats should be soaked in concentrated 4. ___
   A. hydrogen peroxide   B. brine solution
   C. gibberelic acid   D. sulfuric acid
   E. sodium hydroxide

5. Palatable woody vegetation is called   5. ___
   A. forage   B. mast   C. browse   D. pasturage
   E. brush

6. *Which* of the following is the MAIN requirement for a suc-   6. ___
cessful "type conversion?"
   A. Site and plant selection
   B. Removal of nondesired cover
   C. Establishment of a desired adapted species
   D. Soil preparation
   E. Maintenance

7. What is the *most important* sondieration for rejuvenation   7. ___
   treatment projects?
      A. Treat scattered small spots or strips instead of a
         large single area
      B. Gear the amount of forage produced to the number of
         animals who will be using it
      C. Treat areas in a way that the value will be prolonged
         for a long period
      D. Treatments should be rotated so that no one is mani-
         pulated more often than once in 10-20 years
      E. Tailor the program to fit the actual needs of the tar=
         get species

8. What is the *most satisfactory* method of seed testing?   8. ___
      A. Flotation
      B. Checking the growth of the excised embryos
      C. Direct germination success
      D. Biochemical staining of embryos
      E. Measurement of enzyme activity

9. Which of the following are important to the cold stratifica-   9. ___
   tion treatment for breaking internal dormancy of seeds?
       I. A suitable moisture-retaining medium
      II. Seeds should be mixed uniformly with about one-to-three
          times their volume of the medium
     III. Containers of seeds should be subjected to below-freezing
          temperatures for 30-90 days
      IV. Freezing should be followed by cold treatment of around
          40° F. for an additional 30-45 days
       V. After treatment, seeds should be allowed to dry thoroughly
          before planting

   The CORRECT answer is:
      A. I,II   B. I,II,V   C. I,II,III,V   D. III,IV,V
      E. All of the above

10. All of the following are true of prescribed burning EXCEPT: 10. ___
      A. Backfires are recommended where the trees are small
      B. Flankfires are used under larger trees
      C. The best condition is a constant, northerly breeze of
         3-10 mph.
      D. Weather conditions should be constant for a 12-hour
         period
      E. Day burning is preferred for minimum fire intensity

11. What constitutes sleeping or roosting cover?   11. ___
      A. Vegetation offering protection from driving rains and
         snow
      B. Vegetation from which game cannot be driven by pre-
         dators
      C. A place offering shade in summer and wind protection in
         winter
      D. Grassland for some; shrubs or trees for others
      E. Shrubs and trees on knolls or ridges

12. *How* should Bitterbrush be regenerated? By   12. ___
    I. railing   II. dozing   III rolling   IV. roto-cutting
    V. pruning

    The CORRECT answer is:
    A. I,III   B. II,IV   C. I,III,V   D. III,IV,V
    E. IV,V

13. All of the following are characteristics of nonviable seeds 13. ___
    EXCEPT: They are
    A. firm   B. blind   C. filled with resin
    D. rancid   E. thin

14. *Which* of the following are TRUE of rodent predation of   14. ___
    seeds?
      I. Small plots are more vulnerable to seed-loss than
         larger plots
     II. Endrin-Arasan is used as a rodent repellent
    III. Gum-dipped gloves should be used in handling treated
         seeds
     IV. Steep slopes are less vulnerable to seed loss than
         flat plots
      V. Aluminum powder is added to the repellent as a marker
         to attract rodents

    THE CORRECT ANSWER IS:
    A. I,IV   B. II,III,V   C. I,II,III   D. I,II,IV
    E. II,III,IV,V

15. *What* is the MAIN reason for the absence of wildlife in dense 15. ___
    virgin forests?
    A. There is not enough sunlight   B. There is not enough food
    C. There is little empty space
    D. There is inadequate moisture
    E. Ground cover is inadequate

16. Cover for any species *must*   16. ___
    A. provide an escape route
    B. provide adequate food for the trapped species
    C. be dense enough to prevent continued harassment from
       predators
    D. be able to attract and isolate the species
    E. be abundant enough to offset shortages in other locations

17. *What* are the requirements for chaparral-type brushfields   17. ___
    that are targeted for improvement?
      I. More than 20% of the stand should be composed of de-
         sirable browse species
     II. Slope and soil must be favorable
    III. The density of the canopy must be less than 70%
     IV. The average height of the desirable species is less
         than 5 feet
      V. The browse is unavailable or unpalatable due to the
         age of the stand

    The CORRECT answer is:
    A. I,II   B. I,II,V   C. II,IV,V   D. II,III,IV,V
    E. All of the above

18. *What* is the *major* difficulty with the flotation test for seed   18. ___
    viability?
    A. It may be injurious to seeds with thin coats
    B. Most seeds are not so heavy as water
    C. It is unreliable
    D. It is time-consuming
    E. Some seeds are permeable to water

19. *What* are the *principal* benefits of wildlife openings? Clearings19. ___
      I. *furnish* forage for elk,deer,grouse,etc.
     II. *help in* the harvest of elk,deer,and grouse
    III. *provide* nesting sites for turkeys and grouse
     IV. *attract* insects that young birds need for food
      V. *offer* protection from predation

    The CORRECT answer is:
    A. I,III,IV   B. I,II,IV   C. I,III,V   D. II,IV
    E. I,III,IV,V

20. *Which* of the following factors that influence wildlife popula- 20. ___
    tions are the MOST important?
      I. Availability of food
     II. Abundance and effectiveness of predatory species
    III. Competition with other species
     IV. Disease
      V. Presence of cover

    The CORRECT answer is:
    A. I,II   B. I,IV   C. I,V   D. I,II,IV   E. I,III,IV

21. *What* areas should be *excluded* from any sagebrush control pro- 21. ___
    jects?   Areas
      I. of low,sparse sagebrush with a good understory of
         grass and herbs
     II. rarely used by grouse for food or nesting
    III. of low improvement potential
     IV. adjacent to aspen or willows
      V. outside one quarter mile of strutting grounds

    The CORRECT answer is:
    A. I,II,III   B. I,III,IV   C. III,IV,V   D. II,IV,V
    E. All of the above

22. Browseways and openings in chaparrel-type   brushfields are   22. ___
    constructed by all of the following ways EXCEPT:
    A. With dozers   B. With mowers   C. With rollers
    D. With herbicides   E. By prescribed burning

23. All of the following are *true* of direct germination tests   23. ___
    EXCEPT:
    A. Enough water is poured into the container so that the
       medium will absorb its capacity
    B. Temperatures should be kept constant
    C. Moisture levels should be kept constant
    D. Flats should never have watertight bottoms
    E. Light is not necessary

4

24. A protective cover of vegetation provides wildlife with   24. ___
                  cover.
    I. winter   II. refuge   III. loafing
    IV. fawning or nesting   V. sleeping or roosting

    The CORRECT answer is:
    A. I,II   B. III,IV,V   C. II,V   D. I,III,IV
    E. All of the above

25. When overpopulations of game exist, *what* is the FIRST step 25. ___
    that should be taken?
    A. Provide additional food supplies not native to the area
    B. Encourage natural reproduction of food plants native to
       the area
    C. Cut down the numbers of game
    D. Provide additional food supplies of the type found in
       the area
    E. The area should be made unavailable to other wildlife

26. *Which* of the following are guidelines used in juniper- 26. ___
    pinyon clearing projects in order to avoid damage to
    deer and elk habitat?
    I. Leave woody vegetation covering no more than 15% of
       the treated area
   II. Leave live juniper crowns covering 5% of the treated
       area
  III. Do not use control methods which tend to kill deer
       bowse plants
   IV. Treat slopes steeper than 15%
    V. Do not treat northerly exposures

    The CORRECT answer is:
    A. I,II,IV   B. I,II,III   C. III,V   D. II,III,V
    E. I,II,III,IV

27. *What* is the MOST important *first* step in establishing herba-27. ___
    ceous plants?
    A. Timing the seeding
    B. Getting a good cover of seed
    C. Eliminating undesirable competing vegetation
    D. Planting the seeds at the proper depth
    E. Species selection

28. Seeds with seedcoat dormancy that have been successfully 28. ___
    treated appear
    A. glossy   B. pitted   C. shriveled   D. dull   E. moldy

29. The term *escape cover* generally applies to _____ cover. 29. ___
    I. winter   II. refuge   III. loafing
    IV. fawning or nesting   B. steep or roosting

    The CORRECT answer is:
    A. I,II   B. II,IV,V   C. II,V   D. II,IV
    E. II,III,V

30. What is the MOST successful way of reducing herds of big   30. ___
    game?
      A. Eventual starvation from inadequate food supplies
      B. Driving the animals away from concentration areas
      C. Trapping surpluses and removing the animals to under-
         populated. areas
      D. Extending the hunting privileges in heavily populated
         areas
      E. Euthanasia

31. Cover height of herbaceous ground cover is GREATEST for: 31. ___
      A. Hungarian partridge   B. Sharptail grouse
      C. Bobwhite quail   D. Sage grouse
      E. Prairie chicken

32. What is the BEST way to prepare a seedbed for herbaceous   31. ___
    plants? By
      A. burning the site prior to planting
      B. rolling the area with a heavy log or with rubber tires
      C. scalping the site
      D. discing the soil
      E. fertilizing the soil

33. Which of the following are methods to overcome seedcoat   32. ___
    dormancy?
        I. Acid treatment   II. Cold stratification
      III. Warm, followed by cold stratification
       IV. Mechanical stratification
        V. Hotwater treatment

    The CORRECT answer is:
      A. I,III,V   B. I,IV   C. I,IV,V   D. II,III,IV
      E. II,III,V

34. Corridors are used by wildlife for   33. ___
        I. shade   II. shelter   III. loafing cover
       IV. fawning or nesting cover   V. sleep or roosting cover

    The CORRECT answer is:
      A. I,II   B. II,IV,V   C. II,V   D. II,IV   E. II,III,V

35. Which of the following are TRUE of forest openings?   34. ___
        I. Cultivated openings find their value in concentrating
           wildlife during restrocking
       II. Natural openings provide the ecological environment
           under which native game thrive
      III. Cultivated openings must be maintained to prevent re-
           invasion by undesirable plants
       IV. Natural openings are maintained as areas of annual food
           patch plantings
        V. Cultivated openings should include low ground-cover type
           vegetation and shrubs and trees

    The CORRECT answer is:
      A. I,II,V   B. I,II,III   C. III,IV,V   D. II,III,IV
      E. II,III,IV,V

6

36. Den formation is *most directly* due to
    A. the activities of the animal user
    B. decay
    C. the efforts of birds
    D. fortuitous circumstances
    E. the activities of man

36. ___

37. *Which* of the following should guide grain plantings for upland game?
    I. Plots should be irregularly shaped
    II. Plots should be located adjacent to good cover
    III. Plots should be located on steep slopes planted in narrow strips
    IV. Food should be available in late fall to early winter
    V. Plant every year until the grain is fully established

    The CORRECT answer is:
    A. I,II   B. I,II,III   C. I,III   D. I,IV,V
    E. I,II,IV,V

37. ___

38. *Which* of the following are TRUE of internal dormancy of seeds?
    I. It is the most common type of seed dormancy
    II. Germination cannot begin until there are chemical changes in the stored food or embryo
    III. Seeds must be tested to determine the proper corrective method
    IV. Unusually small embryos must be given time to grow before germination is possible
    V. Most embryos do not develop due to lack of water and oxygen

    The CORRECT answer is:
    A. I,III,IV   B. I,II,IV   C. I,IV,V   D. II,IV,V
    E. IV,V

38. ___

39. Den trees are used for
    I. nesting   II. brooding, rearing   III. hibernation
    IV. shelter from the elements   V. seclusion from predators
    The CORRECT answer is:
    A. I,II   B. II,III   C. I,II,III   D. I,II,III,V
    E. All of the above

39. ___

40. *What* MAINLY determines the number and size of forest openings? The
    I. presence of predators
    II. habits of the target wildlife species
    III. size of the wildlife population
    IV. stand density encountered throughout the range
    V. age and size of the stand

    The CORRECT answer is:
    A. I,II   B. II,III   C. I,II,III   D. I,II,III,IV
    E. II,IV

40. ___

41. All of the following require den trees EXCEPT:
    A. Gray and fox squirrels   B. Bluebird
    C. Raccoon   D. Bobwhite quail
    E. Owls

41. ___

7

42. Which of the following grains are valuable for waterfowl,   42. ____
    especially where the site is flooded for part of the year?
      I. Rye   II. Buckwheat   III. Millet   IV. Barley
      V. Sorghum

    The CORRECT answer is:
      A. I,III,V   B. I,II,IV   C. I,III,IV   D. II,III,IV
      E. III,V

43. What is the MOST common method of pre-treating seeds with   43. ____
    impervious coats?
      A. Acid treatment   B. Mechanical stratification
      C. Hotwater treatment   D. Cold stratification
      E. Water, followed by cold stratification

44. What is the PRIMARY advantage of nest boxes? They   44. ____
      A. are economical to build and to maintain
      B. quickly correct den scarcities
      C. are predation-proof
      D. are designed to meet the target species specifications
      E. increase the population of the target species

45. Which of the following are considered to be type conver-   45. ____
    sions of existing cover?
      I. Creation of a permanent treeless opening in a forest
     II. Large brush fields converted to tree plantations
    III. Browse release over a designated area
     IV. Rejuvenation treatments
      V. Modification of the forest composition

    The CORRECT answer is:
      A. I,II,V   B. I,II,III,V   C. I,II   D. III,IV,V
      E. All of the above

46. Which of the following volunteer vegetation around pothole   46. ____
    has duck food value?
      I. Horsetail   II. Bindweed   III. Bulrush
     IV. Bluejoint grass   V. Marsh cinquefoil

    The CORRECT answer is:
      A. I,IV,V   B. I,IV   C. II,III   D. II,III,IV
      E. II,III,IV,V

47. What environment is BEST for most seed storage?   47. ____
      A. Low moisture content and low temperatures
      B. low moisture content and high temperatures
      C. Ordinary air temperature in dry climates
      D. High moisture content and cold temperatures
      E. Temperatures below freezing

48. What is the MOST widely used method of breaking internal   48. ____
    formancy?
      A. Acid treatment   B. Mechanical stratification
      C. Hotwater treatment   D. Chemical treatment
      E. Cold stratification

8

49. *What* are the *basic* requirements of wood duck nest boxes?   49. ___
    I. The opening is large enough
   II. Protection from predators
  III. The base will hold a clutch of eggs
   IV. The box is weatherproof
    V. There is enough debris to form a base and cover
       for the first few eggs

The CORRECT answer is:
    A. I,II   B. I,III,IV   C. I,II,III   D. I,III,V
    E. All of the above

50. *What* are the purposes of *type conversions* of existing   50. ___
   cover? To
    I. *create* favorable interspersions of food and cover
   II. *attract* a target species
  III. *lessen* or *eliminate* predation
   IV. *develop* edge
    V. *provide* openings with herbaceous vegetation in ex-
      tensive areas of dense brush or timber

The CORRECT answer is:
    A. I,IV,V   B. II,III   C. I,II,III   D. I,II,V
    E. I,II,III,V

KEY (CORRECT ANSWERS)

1.	C	11.	E	21.	B	31.	D	41.	D
2.	C	12.	D	22.	E	32.	D	42.	D
3.	B	13.	A	23.	B	33.	C	43.	A
4.	D	14.	C	24.	A	34.	A	44.	B
5.	C	15.	B	25.	C	35.	B	45.	C
6.	A	16.	C	26.	D	36.	B	46.	C
7.	E	17.	B	27.	C	37.	A	47.	A
8.	C	18.	C	28.	D	38.	B	48.	E
9.	A	19.	B	29.	A	39.	E	49.	D
10.	E	20.	C	30.	D	40.	E	50.	A

EXAMINATION SECTION
TEST 1

DIRECTIONS: Each question or incomplete statement is followed by several suggested answers or completions. Select the one that BEST answers the question or completes the statement. *PRINT THE LETTER OF THE CORRECT ANSWER IN THE SPACE AT THE RIGHT.*

1. Each of the following is an example of a biome EXCEPT the   1.___
   A. North American prairie
   B. Grand Canyon
   C. tropical rain forest
   D. grasslands of the sub-Sahara

2. When an aquatic environment experiences an explosion in   2.___
   the population of microorganisms, the organisms later die
   and decompose, causing a chain reaction of death and
   decay until the body of water becomes marshy.
   This process is called
   A. eutrophication   B. putrefaction
   C. aerobiosis   D. biodegradation

3. The total weight of all the living organisms in any given   3.___
   system is called
   A. ecotone   B. biomass
   C. demography   D. census

4. What is the name for an organism, usually a mold or fungus,   4.___
   that consumes the tissue of dead plants or animals?
   A. Parasite   B. Epiphyte
   C. Saprophyte   D. Autotroph

5. The term for an arctic or mountainous area that is too   5.___
   cold to support trees and is vegetated with low mosses
   and grasses is
   A. savanna   B. taiga   C. steppe   D. tundra

6. In a body of water, microscopic free-floating organisms   6.___
   that photosynthesize their own food are called
   A. krill   B. zooplankton
   C. phytoplankton   D. plasma

7. Animals that receive their energy from direct consumption   7.___
   of plant matter are called _____ consumers.
   A. primary   B. secondary
   C. tertiary   D. quaternary

8. Each of the following is one of the principal reasons,   8.___
   imposed by humans, for the extinction of modern species
   EXCEPT
   A. imposed breeding combinations
   B. destruction of habitat
   C. introduction of foreign species
   D. extermination of predators

9. When an ecosystem has reached a final stage of development   9.___
   in which it can only be changed by some outside agent, such
   as the introduction of another species, this is called a
      A. critical level   B. climax community
      C. saturation   D. plateau

10. Which of the following animals are MOST likely to exhibit   10.___
    territorial behaviors?
       A. Large grazing mammals
       B. Small predatory mammals
       C. Fishes
       D. Birds

11. Which of the types of associations below does NOT result   11.___
    in a positive effect for both species involved in the
    relationship?
       A. Symbiosis   B. Commensalism
       C. Parasitism   D. Mutualism

12. A plant (such as moss) that grows on another plant but   12.___
    does not use the host plant for food is called a(n)
       A. osmotroph   B. epiphyte
       C. fungus   D. phagocyte

13. What is the term for organic matter that is in the soil   13.___
    and is characterized by slow decomposition?
       A. Topsoil   B. Substrate
       C. Subsoil   D. Humus

14. Evolution involves changing gene frequencies resulting   14.___
    from each of the following EXCEPT
       A. genetic drift
       B. selection pressure from the environment and inter-
          acting species
       C. learned survival behaviors
       D. recurrent mutations

15. What is the name for a partially enclosed coastal body of   15.___
    shallow water that has a free connection with the open sea?
       A. Delta   B. Estuary   C. Bay   D. Aquifer

16. Autotrophs are organisms that obtain their energy   16.___
       A. directly from the sun
       B. through the consumption of plant matter
       C. through predation of other animals
       D. from decomposing plant and animal tissues

17. When the common gene pool's genetic flow is interrupted   17.___
    by an isolating mechanism, resulting in species diversity
    or the formation of a new species, what natural selection
    process has occurred?
       A. Mutation   B. Speciation
       C. Character displacement   D. Gestation

18. The surface volume of water in the ocean or a large lake that receives enough light to support photosynthesis is called the _____ zone.
    A. benthic
    B. eukaryotic
    C. littoral
    D. euphotic

18.____

19. Which of the following is NOT capable of transforming molecular nitrogen into forms that are usable by living organisms?
    A. Photochemical reactions
    B. Lightning
    C. Specialized bacteria and algae
    D. Atmospheric pressure

19.____

20. What kind of ecosystems GENERALLY characterize temperate areas with low rainfall?
    A. Desert
    B. Prairie
    C. Deciduous forest
    D. Tundra

20.____

21. All the non-living organic matter in an ecosystem is known collectively as
    A. ore   B. plankton   C. detritus   D. particulate

21.____

22. In regions where chemical air pollutants have darkened the surrounding trees, some species of moths adapt by shifting their population's coloring from light to dark. This adaptation is known as
    A. industrial melanism
    B. homeostasis
    C. genetic osmosis
    D. natural succession

22.____

23. In the United States, which of the following species has made the most successful adaptation to the growth and expansion of human populations?
    A. Mountain lion
    B. Bighorn sheep
    C. Deer
    D. Bison

23.____

24. The vertebrate animals that appear FIRST on the evolutionary record are
    A. birds   B. fish   C. reptiles   D. mammals

24.____

25. All organisms that obtain their energy from sources other than sunlight are known collectively as
    A. autotrophs
    B. primary consumers
    C. heterotrophs
    D. omnivores

25.____

KEY (CORRECT ANSWERS)

1. B	6. C	11. C	16. A	21. C
2. A	7. A	12. B	17. B	22. A
3. B	8. A	13. D	18. D	23. C
4. C	9. B	14. C	19. D	24. B
5. D	10. D	15. B	20. B	25. C

TEST 2

DIRECTIONS: Each question or incomplete statement is followed by several suggested answers or completions. Select the one that BEST answers the question or completes the statement. *PRINT THE LETTER OF THE CORRECT ANSWER IN THE SPACE AT THE RIGHT.*

1. Dystrophic lakes are characterized by which of the following conditions?
   A. High concentrations of calcium and oxygen
   B. Inadequate decomposition of matter
   C. Lack of photosynthetic organisms
   D. Large number and variety of organisms

   1.____

2. Which of the animals below is generally considered to have the LEAST complex social order among members of its species?
   A. African lion
   B. Honeybee
   C. North American alligator
   D. Canada goose

   2.____

3. The taiga is the
   A. coniferous forest of the northern latitudes of North America
   B. scrub desert of Southwestern North America
   C. temperate deciduous forest of Eurasia
   D. subtropical grasslands of Africa

   3.____

4. The uppermost trees on a mountain slope inhabit an area known as the
   A. Longren   B. tundra   C. humus   D. Krummholz

   4.____

5. Which of the following organisms is likely to be MORE abundant in a swiftly-moving stream than in a slow stream?
   A. Phytoplankton   B. Fish
   C. Crayfish   D. Zooplankton

   5.____

6. A wheat field has an inherent ability to support more locusts than a short-grass prairie.
   Therefore, it is said to have a _____ for locusts.
   A. commensal requirement
   B. greater environmental resistance
   C. more limiting habitat
   D. larger carrying capacity

   6.____

7. The place where wildlife lives is called
   A. habitat   B. pasture   C. home   D. tundra

   7.____

8. The unique function of a particular species, along with
   its habitat, are known together as its   8.___
   A. home range   B. critical level
   C. ecotone   D. ecological niche

9. Which of the types of wild species below probably has the   9.___
   LOWEST risk of extinction in the modern world?
   A. Highly specialized or immobile organisms
   B. Animals that aggregate and migrate in large groups
   C. Large grazing animals
   D. Large carnivorous predators

10. With what kind of species association do wild rose bushes   10.___
    and mountain lions interact?
    A. Competition   B. Parasitism
    C. Neutralism   D. Mutualism

11. Which of the bird species below is currently the LEAST   11.___
    endangered in the United States?
    A. Bald eagle   B. Ivory-billed woodpecker
    C. California condor   D. Whooping crane

12. When populations of differing species become dependent on   12.___
    each other for survival, the relationship is described as
    A. neutralism   B. mutualism
    C. unibiosis   D. parasitism

13. Which of the organisms below is an example of an ungulate?   13.___
    A. Rhesus monkey   B. Kodiak bear
    C. Tule elk   D. Cheetah

14. Large North American carnivores such as the timber wolf   14.___
    and the black bear generally prey upon the same types of
    animal species.
    Therefore, they are said to share the same
    A. habitat   B. food chain
    C. ecological niche   D. trophic level

15. Which is the LIKELIEST result of overcrowding on a   15.___
    species population?
    A. Immediate adaptation
    B. Forced migration
    C. An explosion in predation
    D. Reduced reproductive yield

16. Respiration that takes place without the presence of   16.___
    oxygen is described as
    A. antibiotic   B. carbonic
    C. anaerobic   D. unsaturated

17. Environmental resistance is the   17.___
    A. natural resilience of the environment to disturbances
       from outside sources
    B. tendency of ecosystems to remain the same over a
       period of time

C. environmental interactions which collectively inhibit the growth of a species
D. worldwide industrial practices that repeatedly damage the natural environment

18. Which of the animals below is characterized by a matri-archal social order?
    A. African elephant   B. Mountain gorilla
    C. Caribou   D. American bald eagle

19. In the months after lava flow has cooled and settle on a Hawaiian island, the area is gradually populated by ferns and lichens.
    Which successional stage does this represent?
    A. Primary   B. Secondary   C. Tertiary   D. Quaternary

20. With what kind of species association do intertidal barnacles and mussels interact?
    A. Competition   B. Parasitism
    C. Neutralism   D. Mutualism

21. Which of the following ecosystems below is an example of a climax system?
    A(n)
    A. woodland meadow   B. old-growth redwood forest
    C. inland marsh   D. small wooded pond

22. In a climate that is milder than that of the coniferous forest, where rainfall is abundant relative to evapora-tion, what kind of ecological community would be MOST likely?
    A. Tundra   B. Tallgrass prairie
    C. Short-grass prairie D. Deciduous forest

23. The middle waters of a lake, where oxygen content falls off rapidly with depth, are the
    A. hypolimnion   B. benthic zone
    C. thermocline   D. euphotic zone

24. The control mechanisms within an ecosystem that maintain constancy by resisting external stresses are known collectively as
    A. homeostasis   B. contrapuntal mechanisms
    C. environmental resistance D. heterotrophic modulation

25. Biotic potential is the
    A. largest possible size of an individual organism
    B. range of adaptive flexibility for an organism in a given environment
    C. maximum rate of growth for a species population
    D. range of possibilities for an evolving ecosystem

KEY (CORRECT ANSWERS)

1. B			11. A	
2. C			12. B	
3. A			13. C	
4. D			14. B	
5. C			15. D	
6. D			16. C	
7. A			17. C	
8. D			18. A	
9. B			19. A	
10. C			20. A	

21. B
22. D
23. C
24. A
25. C

———

EXAMINATION SECTION
TEST 1

DIRECTIONS: Each question or incomplete statement is followed by several suggested answers or completions. Select the one that BEST answers the question or completes the statement. *PRINT THE LETTER OF THE CORRECT ANSWER IN THE SPACE AT THE RIGHT.*

1. During an interview with a witness, the investigator should carefully observe the witness's gestures and facial expressions.
   To interpret the meaning of these actions, the investigator should do all of the following EXCEPT to

   A. try to *read* the situation in which a puzzling gesture is used
   B. ask questions that relate specifically to the gesture
   C. take an educated guess based on past experience
   D. rely on the standard meaning of the gesture

   1._____

2. Of the following, the MOST important skill for a supervisor of investigators to possess is the ability to

   A. communicate effectively
   B. obtain the respect of his staff
   C. remain calm in pressure situations
   D. develop high morale among his subordinates

   2._____

3. Following are three statements concerning the preparation by an investigator of a written statement taken from a witness:
   I. Have each page initialed by the witness
   II. Correct and initial any mistakes in grammar that are made by the witness
   III. Leave space between paragraphs to facilitate the addition of notes and comments.
   Which of the following correctly classifies the above statements into those that are valid and those that are not?

   A. I is valid, but II and III are not.
   B. II and III are valid, but I is not.
   C. III is valid, but I and II are not.
   D. I and II are valid, but III is not.

   3._____

4. Assume, as an investigator, you are questioning an employee of your agency suspected of misstating previous work experience on his employment application. You notice that the employee is reluctant to admit that his previous statements were inaccurate.
   The one of the following that is the BEST method of obtaining the truth from this employee would be for you to

   A. tell him that his job is not in jeopardy
   B. make him feel he is not being criticized
   C. have him discuss the matter with your supervisor
   D. allow him to correct any inaccuracies on his employment application

   4._____

5. If several witnesses describing the same occurrence agree on most details, the investi-   5.___
   gator should then

   A. determine whether or not these witnesses were in communication with each other
   B. assume that such agreement means that the recollection was correct
   C. assume that the witnesses' observations were incorrect since two or more people
      usually will not agree on the same details
   D. question the witnesses again, concentrating on the details on which they differ

6. In trying to obtain a statement from a hospitalized individual who is unable to receive vis-   6.___
   itors, it would be BEST for an investigator

   A. draw up a statement from his own knowledge of the case and ask a hospital staff
      member to have the patient sign the statement when he is well
   B. contact the patient's family and arrange for an appointment to see the patient as
      soon as his condition permits
   C. leave a message at the hospital for the patient to contact him when he is available
      to receive visitors
   D. appear at the hospital with proper identification and request official permission
      from the hospital administrator to speak with the patient

7. Among employment specialists, it is generally agreed that the value of character refer-   7.___
   ences on employment applications is

   A. *limited,* chiefly because such references are written only by personal friends of the
      applicant
   B. *significant,* chiefly because information they transmit is unavailable from other
      sources
   C. *limited,* chiefly because they tend to give only favorable information
   D. *significant,* chiefly because they have direct knowledge of the applicant's abilities

8. The MOST important requirement of a person who is testifying about a criminal act that   8.___
   he witnessed is that he

   A. was conscious and attentive during the crime
   B. is a respected and trustworthy member of the community
   C. is without a prior criminal record
   D. gives a consistent account of the details of the crime

9. Assume that, after taking a written statement from Employee A, an investigator is about   9.___
   to obtain his signature. He wants to ask Employee B, a co-worker, to witness the signing
   but Employee B is not available at that time.
   To expedite the investigation, it would be MOST desirable for the investigator to

   A. have Employee A sign the statement and obtain Employee B's signature at a later
      time
   B. ask an available disinterested party to witness Employee A's signature
   C. witness Employee A's signature himself
   D. have Employee A sign when Employee B is available

10. Witnesses are usually MOST willing to discuss an event when they are   10._____

   A. disinterested in the subsequent investigation
   B. interviewed immediately following the event
   C. interviewed for the first time
   D. known by the investigator

11. To determine the former addresses of a person who has moved several times within the   11._____
    same locality, it would be BEST to contact

   A. the Post Office   B. insurance companies
   C. public utilities   D. banking institutions

12. The one of the following that is CHARACTERISTIC of the interview as compared with the   12._____
    observation approach to investigation is that an interview generally

   A. requires more time to complete adequately
   B. is more likely to result in incomplete information
   C. is less applicable to the study of an individual's beliefs and values
   D. is less costly to conduct

13. The use of slang on the part of an investigator when questioning subjects is generally   13._____

   A. *inadvisable*; chiefly because it leads to misinterpretations
   B. *advisable*; chiefly because it will insure objective responses
   C. *inadvisable*; chiefly because it can compromise the investigator's dignity
   D. *advisable*; chiefly because it can promote ease of speech and understanding

14. Assume that a job applicant claims on his employment application that he has just   14._____
    recently become a United States citizen.
    Of the following, it would be MOST appropriate for you, in verifying this matter, to con-
    sult the

   A. Department of State   B. Treasury Department
   C. Immigration and Naturalization Service   D. Department of Justice

15. If an investigator receives an anonymous phone call from a person claiming to have   15._____
    knowledge of criminal behavior in an agency which is currently being investigated, the
    investigator should

   A. listen politely and make notes on the important facts given by the informant
   B. tell the informant what has already been discovered and ask if he has anything to
      add
   C. question the informant to obtain all the information he has
   D. ask the informant to submit his information in writing

16. When interviewing a child, an investigator should keep in mind the fact that children   16._____

   A. are psychologically incapable of giving an accurate statement
   B. usually have faulty perception
   C. are easily led into making incorrect statements since they tend to agree with the
      questioner
   D. will often make statements which are pure fantasy because they are not as obser-
      vant as adults

17. Following are three statements concerning the use of an investigator's notebook in court: 17.___
    I.   A looseleaf-type notebook creates a more favorable impression in the court-room than a bound notebook because the former permits the removal of pages unrelated to the case in question
    II. An investigator's notebook should be written in ink, not pencil, because of the need for permanence
    III. The notebook should ideally contain the notes of only one investigation so that its scrutiny will not involve the disclosure of information relating to other investigations
Which of the following CORRECTLY classifies the above statements into those which are valid and those which are not valid?

    A. I and III are valid, but II is not.
    B. I and II are valid, but III is not.
    C. I is valid, but II and III are not.
    D. II and III are valid, but I is not.

18. The first three digits of a social security number are coded for the 18.___

    A. age of the cardholder when the card was issued
    B. cardholder's initials
    C. year the card was issued
    D. area in which the card was issued

19. Two methods of obtaining personal background information are the personal interview 19.___
and the telephone inquiry.
As compared with the latter, the personal type of interview USUALLY _____ flexibility in questioning _____ frankness.

    A. permits; but discourages
    B. restricts; but encourages
    C. permits; and encourages
    D. restricts; and discourages

20. One of the important functions of investigators is to perform surveillances without the 20.___
knowledge of the subject. If a subject thinks he is being followed, he is LEAST likely to react by

    A. reversing his course to see whether anyone else does likewise
    B. boarding a subway car and getting off just before it pulls out
    C. attempting to pass the surveillant several times to view him face-to-face
    D. using the services of a *convoy* to observe whether he is being followed

21. Assume that you are conducting an interview with a prospective employee who is of lim- 21.___
ited mental ability and low socio-economic status.
Of the following, it is MOST likely that asking him many open-ended questions about his work experience would cause him to respond

    A. articulately   B. reluctantly
    C. comfortably   D. aggressively

22. Assume, as an investigator, you want a witness to sign a statement. 22._____
Which of the following phrases is MOST likely to secure his signature?

    A. I would appreciate it if you would sign the statement at this time.
    B. Sign the statement where indicated.
    C. Sign the statement when you get the chance.
    D. If the statement is generally correct, please sign it.

23. During an interview, a subject makes statements an investigator knows to be false. 23._____
Of the following, it would be MOST appropriate for the investigator to

    A. point out each inconsistency in the subject's story as soon as the investigator detects it
    B. interrupt the subject and request that he submit to a polygraph test
    C. allow the subject to continue talking until he becomes enmeshed in his lies and then confront him with his falsehoods
    D. allow the subject to finish what he has to say and then explicitly inform him that it is a crime to lie to a government employee

24. One of the major objectives of a pre-employment interview is to get the interviewee to 24._____
respond freely to inquiries. The one of the following actions that would be MOST likely to
restrict the conversation of the interviewee would be for the investigator to

    A. keep a stenographic record of the interviewee's statements
    B. ask questions requiring complete explanations
    C. pose direct, specific questions to the interviewee
    D. allow the interviewee to respond to questions at his own pace

25. A list of the names, addresses, and titles of city employees is made available to the pub- 25._____
lic by the

    A. civil service commission
    B. comptroller's office
    C. mayor's office
    D. municipal reference and research center

KEY (CORRECT ANSWERS)

1.	D		11.	C
2.	A		12.	D
3.	A		13.	D
4.	B		14.	C
5.	A		15.	C
6.	B		16.	C
7.	C		17.	D
8.	A		18.	D
9.	B		19.	C
10.	B		20.	C

21.	B
22.	B
23.	C
24.	A
25.	D

———

READING COMPREHENSION
UNDERSTANDING AND INTERPRETING WRITTEN MATERIAL
EXAMINATION SECTION
TEST 1

DIRECTIONS: Each question or incomplete statement is followed by several suggested answers or completions. Select the one that BEST answers the question or completes the statement. *PRINT THE LETTER OF THE CORRECT ANSWER IN THE SPACE AT THE RIGHT.*

Questions 1-5.

DIRECTIONS: Questions 1 through 5 are based on the following passage. You are to answer the questions which follow based SOLELY upon the information in the passage.

More than 700 dolphins and whales piled up on France's Atlantic coast last February and March. Most were common dolphins, but the toll also included striped and bottlenose dolphins — even a few harbor porpoises and fin, beaked, pilot, and minke whales. Many victims had ropes around their tails or had heads or tails cut off; some had been partly butchered for food. To scientists the cause is obvious: These marine mammals were seen as waste, *byaatah,* to the fishermen who snared them in their nets while seeking commercial fish.

Mid-water trawlers are responsible for this, not drift nets, says Anne Collet, a French biologist who examined the carcasses. The European Union has banned large drift nets. Two other European treaties call for bycatch reduction by vessels using huge trawls for hake and other species. But the Bay of Biscay falls beyond the treaties, a painfully obvious loophole.

1.   What killed the dolphins and whales at the Bay of Biscay?   1.____

    A.   The propellers of recreational motorboats
    B.   Fishermen using drift nets to catch commercial fish
    C.   Fishermen seeking commercial fish
    D.   Fishermen seeking their tails and heads as trophies

2.   What is *bycatch?*   2.____

    A.   Animals accidentally caught in the same nets used to catch other types of fish
    B.   Animals which typically gather close to certain types of fish, allowing fishermen to hunt more than one species at a time
    C.   Those parts of animals and fish discarded by fishermen after the catch
    D.   Those fish which exceed the fisherman's specified limit and must be thrown back

3.   The dolphins and whales were killed around the Bay of Biscay because the   3.____

    A.   treaties which protect these species of dolphins and whales do not reach the Bay of Biscay
    B.   bodies of the animals were dumped at the Bay of Biscay, but scientists do not know where they were killed
    C.   treaties which limit the use of drift nets do not reach the Bay of Biscay
    D.   treaties which limit the use of trawls do not reach the Bay of Biscay

4. Where is the Bay of Biscay located?   4.___

    A. France's Pacific coast
    B. France's Atlantic coast
    C. The European Union's Atlantic coast
    D. The French Riviera

5. What types of fish are mid-water trawlers usually used for?   5.___

    A. Common, striped, and bottlenose dolphins
    B. Common dolphins, harbor porpoises, and pilot whales
    C. Hake and pilot, minke, fin, and beaked whales
    D. Hake and other species

Questions 6-10.

DIRECTIONS: Questions 6 through 10 are based on the following passage. You are to answer the questions which follow based SOLELY upon the information in the passage.

Malaria once infected 9 out of 10 people in North Borneo, now known as Brunei. In 1955, the World Health Organization (WHO) began spraying the island with dieldrin (a DDT relative) to kill malaria-carrying mosquitoes. The program was so successful that the dread disease was virtually eliminated.

Other, unexpected things began to happen, however. The dieldrin also killed other insects, including flies and cockroaches living in houses. At first, the islanders applauded this turn of events, but then small lizards that also lived in the houses died after gorging themselves on dieldrin-contaminated insects. Next, cats began dying after feeding on the lizards. Then, in the absence of cats, rats flourished and overran the villages. Now that the people were threatened by sylvatic plague carried by rat fleas, WHO parachuted healthy cats onto the island to help control the rats.

Then the villagers' roofs began to fall in. The dieldrin had killed wasps and other insects that fed on a type of caterpillar that either avoided or was not affected by the insecticide. With most of its predators eliminated, the caterpillar population exploded, munching its way through its favorite food: the leaves used in thatched roofs.

Ultimately, this episode ended happily: Both malaria and the unexpected effects of the spraying program were brought under control. Nevertheless, the chain of unforeseen events emphasizes the unpredictability of interfering in an ecosystem.

6. The World Health Organization (WHO) began spraying dieldrin on North Borneo in order   6.___
  to

    A. kill the bacteria which causes malaria
    B. kill the mosquitoes that carry malaria
    C. disrupt the foodchain so that malaria-carrying mosquitoes would die
    D. kill the mosquitoes, flies, and cockroaches that carry malaria

7. Which of the following did the dieldrin kill?   7._____

    A. Mosquitoes   B. Rats
    C. Caterpillars   D. All of the above

8. The villagers' roofs caved in because the dieldrin killed   8._____

    A. mosquitoes, flies, rats, and cats
    B. the trees whose leaves are used in thatched roofs
    C. the caterpillar that eats the leaves used in thatched roofs
    D. the predators of the caterpillar that eats the leaves used in thatched roofs

9. Which of the following was NOT a side effect of spraying dieldrin on Borneo?   9._____

    A. Malaria was virtually eliminated.
    B. The rat population exploded.
    C. The cat population exploded.
    D. The caterpillar population exploded.

10. Why did the World Health Organization (WHO) deliver healthy cats to Borneo without try-   10._____
    ing to replenish the other animals and insects which had been wiped out by the dieldrin?
    The

    A. presence of a healthy cat population was all that was required to restore the bal-
        anced ecosystem
    B. rats that cats preyed upon carried an illness threatening to humans
    C. other insects and animals killed by the dieldrin were nuisances and the villagers
        were happy to be free of them
    D. villagers' had become attached to cats as domestic pets

Questions 11-15.

DIRECTIONS: Questions 11 through 15 are based on the following passage. You are to
                  answer the questions which follow based SOLELY upon the information in the
                  passage.

    Historically, towns and cities grew as a natural byproduct of people choosing to live in
certain areas for agricultural, business, or recreational reasons. Beginning in the 1920s, pri-
vate and governmental planners began to think about how an ideal town would be planned.
These communities would be completely built before houses were offered for sale. This concept of preplanning, designing, and building an ideal town was not fully developed until the
1960s. By 1976, about forty-three towns could be classified as planned *new towns*.

    One example of a new town is Reston, Virginia, located about 40 kilometers west of
Washington, D.C. Reston began to accept residents in 1964 and has a projected population
of eighty thousand. Because developers tried to preserve the great natural beauty of the area
and the high quality of architectural design of its buildings, Reston has attracted much attention. Reston also has innovative programs in education, government, transportation, and recreation. For example, the stores in Reston are within easy walking distance of the residential
parts of the community, and there are many open spaces for family activities. Because Reston is not dependent upon the automobile, noise and air pollution have been greatly reduced.
Recent research indicates that the residents of Reston have rated their community much
higher than residents of less well-planned suburbs.

11. When did the concept of first building a town and then offering houses for sale fully develop?   11.____

    A.   1920s   B.   1950s   C.   1960s   D.   1970s

12. The goal of planners who develop and build ideal towns and suburbs is to   12.____

    A.   eliminate the tendency of towns and cities to naturally develop around business or recreational centers
    B.   control population growth
    C.   regulate the resources devoted to housing and recreation
    D.   cut down on suburban sprawl by developing communities where residents are not dependent on cars to maintain a high quality of living

13. Which of the following goals did developers have in mind when planning the community of Reston?   13.____
    I.   Preservation of natural beauty
    II.   Communal living spaces
    III.   Communal recreational spaces
    IV.   High standards of architectural design

The CORRECT answer is:

    A.   I, II, III, IV   B.   I, III, IV
    C.   II, III, IV   D.   I, II, IV

14. The fact that stores in Reston are within easy walking distance of the residential parts of the community is an example of innovation in   14.____

    A.   transportation   B.   recreation
    C.   education   D.   all of the above

15. What are the environmental advantages to towns like Reston?   15.____

    A.   Uniform architecture
    B.   Individual recreational spaces cut down on the overuse of resources
    C.   Decreased noise and air pollution
    D.   Ability to control the number and type of residents

Questions 16-20.

DIRECTIONS: Questions 16 through 20 are based on the following passage. You are to answer the questions which follow based SOLELY upon the information in the passage.

Lead is one of the most common toxic (harmful or poisonous) metals in the intercity environment. It is found, to some extent, in all parts of the urban environment (e.g., air, soil, and older pipes and paint) and in all biological systems, including people. There is no apparent biologic need for lead, but it is sufficiently concentrated in the blood and bones of children living in inner cities to cause health and behavior problems. In some populations over *20%* of the children have levels of lead concentrated in their blood above that believed safe. Lead affects nearly every system of the body. Acute lead toxicity may be characterized by a variety of symptoms, including anemia, mental retardation, palsy, coma, seizures, apathy, uncoordination, subtle loss of recently acquired skills, and bizarre behavior. Lead toxicity is particularly a problem for young children who tend to be exposed to higher concentrations in some urban areas and apparently are more susceptible to lead poisoning than are adults. Following exposure to lead and having acute toxic response, some children manifest aggressive, difficult to manage behavior.

The occurrence of lead toxicity or lead poisoning has cultural, political, and sociological implications. Over 2,000 years ago, the Roman Empire produced and used tremendous amounts of lead for a period of several hundred years. Production rates were as high as 55,000 metric tons per year. Romans had a wide variety of uses for lead, including pots in which grapes were crushed and processed into a syrup for making wine, cups, and goblets from which the wine was drunk, as a base for cosmetics and medicines, and finally for the wealthy class of people who had running water in their homes, lead was used to make the pipes that carried the water. It has been argued by some historians that gradual lead poisoning among the upper class in Rome was partly responsible for Rome's eventual fall.

16. In which parts of the urban environment can lead be found?   16._____
      I. Air
     II. Water
    III. Adults
    IV. Children
The CORRECT answer is:

    A. I, II, III   B. I, III, IV
    C. II, III, IV   D. All of the above

17. Lead toxicity has the most powerful effect on which of the following?   17._____

    A. Mentally retarded children
    B. Young children
    C. Anemic women
    D. Children who suffer from seizures

18. Romans used lead in which of the following?   18._____

    A. Cosmetics   B. Paint   C. Wine   D. Clothes

19. Humans require a certain level of lead in the bloodstream in order to avoid which of the   19._____
following?

    A. Anemia
    B. Uncoordination
    C. Seizures
    D. Scientists have found no biological need for lead among humans

20. Which of the following would most directly support the theory that lead poisoning was   20._____
partially responsible for the fall of Rome?

    A. Evidence of bizarre behavior among ancient Roman leaders
    B. Evidence of lead in the drinking water of ancient Rome
    C. Studies analyzing the lead content of bones of ancient Romans which detect increased levels of lead
    D. Evidence of lead in the environment of ancient Rome

Questions 21-25.

DIRECTIONS: Questions 21 through 25 are based on the following passage. You are to answer the questions which follow based SOLELY upon the information in the passage.

The city of Venice, Italy has been known to be slowly sinking, but for a long time no one knew the cause or a solution. Floods were becoming more and more common, especially during the winter storms when the winds drove waters from the Adriatic Sea into the city's streets. Famous for its canals and architectural beauty, Venice was in danger of being destroyed by the very lagoon that had sustained its commerce for more than a thousand years. Then the reason that the city was sinking was discovered: groundwater in the region was being pumped out and used; the depletion of the water table, over time, caused the soil to compress under the weight of the city above it. The wells that influenced Venice, which were located on the Italian mainland as well as on the islands that make up Venice, supplied water to nearly industrial and domestic users.

Once the cause was discovered, the wells were capped .and other sources of water were found; as a result the city has stopped sinking. This is an example of the application of scientific research on the environment to achieve a solution helpful to a major city.

21. What causes the winter floods in Venice?

    A. The disintegration of the canals that used to protect the city from the floods
    B. Storms that drive waters from the wells into the streets
    C. The flawed canal system for which the city is famous
    D. Storms that drive waters from the Adriatic Sea into the streets

21._____

22. Venice was sinking because of depletion of the

    A. lagoon upon which the city was founded
    B. wells used to flood the lagoons
    C. water table beneath the city
    D. soil beneath the city

22._____

23. What was the water beneath Venice used for?

    A. Wastewater
    B. To supply water to the famous canals
    C. To supply drinking water to Venetians
    D. To supply local industrial users

23._____

24. How was the problem remedied?

    A. City leaders regulated use of the wells and found other sources of water.
    B. The wells were capped.
    C. Flood water was diverted back to the Adriatic Sea.
    D. The wells were used to supply water to nearby industrial and domestic users.

24._____

25. How were scientists able to restore Venice to its proper (and previous) elevation?   25.____

    A.   Venice was not restored to its previous elevation
    B.   By diverting water back into the soil beneath Venice
    C.   By capping the wells and finding other sources of water
    D.   By restoring the water table

———

KEY (CORRECT ANSWERS)

1.	C	11.	C
2.	A	12.	D
3.	D	13.	B
4.	B	14.	A
5.	D	15.	C
6.	B	16.	D
7.	A	17.	B
8.	D	18.	A
9.	C	19.	D
10.	B	20.	C

21.	D
22.	C
23.	D
24.	B
25.	A

———

TEST 2

DIRECTIONS: Each question or incomplete statement is followed by several suggested answers or completions. Select the one that BEST answers the question or completes the statement. *PRINT THE LETTER OF THE CORRECT ANSWER IN THE SPACE AT THE RIGHT.*

Questions 1-5.

DIRECTIONS: Questions 1 through 5 are based on the following passage. You are to answer the questions which follow based SOLELY upon the information in the passage.

China, with one-fifth of the world's population, is the most populous country in the world. Between 1980 and 1995, China's population grew by 200 million people — about three-fourths of the population of the United States — to reach 1.2 billion. Although its growth rate is expected to slow somewhat in the coming decades, population experts predict that there will be 1.5 billion Chinese by 2025. But can China's food production continue to keep pace with its growing population? Should China develop a food deficit, it may need to import more grain from other countries than those countries can spare from their own needs.

To give some idea of the potential impact of China on the world's food supply, consider the following examples. All of the grain produced by Norway would be needed to supply two more beers to each person in China. If the Chinese were to eat as much fish as the Japanese do, China would consume the entire world fish catch. Food for all the chickens required for China to reach its goal of 200 eggs per person per year by 2010 will equal all the grain exported by Canada — the world's second largest grain exporter. Increased demand by China for world grain supplies could result in dramatic increases in food prices and precipitate famines in other areas of the world.

1. China's population increased between 1980 and 1995 by

    A. 200 million people
    B. 1.2 billion people
    C. 1.5 billion people
    D. one-fifth of the world's population

1.____

2. If China developed a food deficit, which of the following would most negatively affect the world's supply of food?

    A. Famines resulting from the increased price of grain
    B. Domestic increase in the production of grain to meet the needs of the Chinese people
    C. International increase in the production of grain to meet China's need
    D. Importing more grain from other countries than those countries could spare

2.____

3. Which of the following was a goal the Chinese government hoped to reach by 2010?

    A. Importing Canada's entire supply of grain
    B. Supplying 200 eggs annually to every citizen
    C. A population of 1.5 billion people
    D. Supplying enough fish to each citizen to match Japan's consumption

3.____

4. Which of the following countries exports the most grain?   4.____

    A. China   B. Norway   C. Canada   D. Japan

5. Which of the following groups contains 200 million people?   5.____

    A. The current population of the United States
    B. Three-quarters of the population of the United States
    C. China's current population
    D. Three-quarters of the population of China

Questions 6-10.

DIRECTIONS: Questions 6 through 10 are based on the following passage. You are to answer the questions which follow based SOLELY upon the information in the passage.

On Tuesday, 16 June 1987, the last dusky seaside sparrow *(Ammo-dramus maratimus nigrescens)* died in captivity at Walt Disney World's Discovery Island Zoological Park in Orlando, Florida. The bird was a male that was probably about twelve years old. Originally, this subspecies and several other subspecies were found in the coastal salt marshes on the Atlantic coast of Florida. (A subspecies is a distinct population of a species that has several characteristics that distinguish it from other populations.) One other subspecies, the Smyrna seaside sparrow *(Ammodramus maratimus pelonata)*, is believed to have become extinct several years ago, and a third subspecies, the Cape Sable seaside sparrow *(Ammodramus maratimus mirabilis)*, was listed as an endangered species in 1967. Before the deaths of the last remaining dusky seaside sparrows, a few males were crossed with another subspecies, Scott's seaside sparrow *(Ammodramus maratimus peninsulae)*. Thus, the hybrid offspring between these two subspecies contain some of the genes that made the dusky seaside sparrow unique.

The endangerment and extinction of these different birds was a direct result of the land development and drainage that destroyed the salt-marsh habitat to which they were adapted. The development of Cape Canaveral as a major center for the U.S. space program also resulted in the modification of much of the birds' original habitat and was a partial cause of their extinction.

6. Which of the following subspecies is NOT yet extinct?   6.____

    A. Dusky seaside sparrow
    B. Cape Sable seaside sparrow
    C. Smyrna seaside sparrow
    D. All of the listed subspecies are extinct

7. A subspecies is a population   7.____

    A. within a species that has been crossed with another population within the same species in order to avoid extinction
    B. within a subspecies that has distinguishing characteristics
    C. that has distinguishing characteristics
    D. within a species that has distinguishing characteristics

8. What was the dusky seaside sparrow's natural habitat?

    A. Coastal salt marshes of Florida
    B. Man-made parks and zoos such as Discovery Land
    C. Flat, desert-like plains around Cape Canaveral
    D. Areas of land development

8.___

9. A hybrid is an animal that

    A. cannot reproduce
    B. is extinct
    C. is the result of a cross between two subspecies
    D. is the result of a cross between two species

9.___

10. What caused the extinction of the dusky seaside sparrow?

    A. An overabundance of predators caused by human influence and development
    B. Destruction of its natural habitat by human development
    C. Inability to reproduce in captivity
    D. All of the above

10.___

Questions 11-15.

DIRECTIONS: Questions 11 through 15 are based on the following passage. You are to answer the questions which follow based SOLELY upon the information in the passage.

For more than 600 years only Adelie penguins lived along the chilly shores of the Western Antarctic Peninsula in the Palmer region. Ornithologist and paleontologist Steven Emslie of the University of North Carolina, Wilmington, found Adelie bones in nests near Palmer Station dating from as early as the 14th century.

But two other penguin species have moved in, apparently as the result of a 50-year warming trend that has seen winter temperatures rise seven to nine degrees F and lessened the amount of ice around the peninsula. *Adelies require the edges of pack ice for foraging,* Emslie says. As the ice shrinks, he believes, their numbers decline. Chinstrap penguins, which forage in the open ocean and aren't affected by ice breakup, began to arrive in the 1950s. Gentoos, normally a subantarctic species, first appeared here in 1975. The two newcomers now form a major portion of the region's penguin population.

11. When did new penguin species begin arriving in the Palmer region?

    A. 1400s   B. 1950s   C. 1975   D. 1990s

11.___

12. Which of the following penguin species are NOT affected by ice breakup?

    A. Adelie   B. Gentoos   C. Chinstrap   D. Emslie

12.___

13. What has caused the new penguin species to move into the Palmer region?

    A. A warming trend
    B. An increase in the amount of pack ice around the peninsula
    C. An increase in the availability of food
    D. All of the above

13.___

14. Adelie penguins have lived in the Palmer region since   14.____

    A.   the 14th century   B.   the early 1900s
    C.   the 1950s   D.   1975

15. What effect does the decrease in the amount of pack ice have on Adelie penguins?   15.____

    A.   Decreased ability to fight off predators
    B.   Increased ability to fight off predators
    C.   Increased ability to forage for food
    D.   Decreased ability to forage for food

Questions 16-20.

DIRECTIONS: Questions 16 through 20 are based on the following passage. You are to answer the questions which follow based SOLELY upon the information in the passage.

The price of a liter of gasoline is determined by two major factors: (1) the cost of purchasing and processing crude oil into gasoline, and (2) various taxes. Most of the differences in gasoline prices between countries are a result of the differences in taxes and reflect differences in government policy toward motor vehicle transportation.

A major objective of governments is to collect money to build and repair roads, and governments often charge the user by taxing the fuel used by the car or truck. Governments can also discourage the use of automobiles by increasing the cost of fuel. An increase in fuel costs also creates a demand for increased fuel efficiency in all forms of motor transport.

Many European countries raise more money from fuel taxes than they spend on building and repairing roads, while the United States raises approximately 60 percent of the moneys needed for roads from fuel taxes. The relatively low cost of fuel in the United States encourages more travel and increases road repair costs. The cost of taxes to the United States consumer is about 20 percent of the cost of fuel, while in Japan and many European countries, the percentage is 60 to 75 percent.

16. Which of the following is likely to result from an increase in the cost of fuel?   16.____

    A.   *Decreased* fuel efficiency
    B.   *Increased* fuel efficiency
    C.   *Increased* travel
    D.   *Increased* road repair costs

17. Which of the following affects the price of gasoline?   17.____

    A.   Cost of purchasing crude oil
    B.   Cost of processing crude oil
    C.   Taxes
    D.   All of the above

18. Most governments tax car and truck fuel in order to   18.____

    A.   finance the costs of repairing roads
    B.   discourage motor travel as much as possible

C. finance various social welfare programs
D. finance public transportation systems

19. Differences in _____ accounts for the differences in gasoline prices between countries.   19.___

   A. the cost of purchasing a car
   B. the amount of crude oil each country exports
   C. government taxes
   D. the number of automobiles imported by individual countries

20. Which of the following is most likely to discourage travel?   20.___

   A. *Decrease* in fuel tax
   B. *Increase* in fuel tax
   C. *Decrease* in fuel efficiency
   D. *Increase* in road repair

Questions 21-25.

DIRECTIONS: Questions 21 through 25 are based on the following passage. You are to answer the questions which follow based SOLELY upon the information in the passage.

Wyoming rancher Jack Turnell is one of a new breed of cowpuncher who gets along with environmentalists. He talks about riparian ecology and biodiversity as fluently as he talks about cattle. *I guess I have learned how to bridge the gap between the environmentalists, the bureaucracies, and the ranching industry.*

Turnell grazes cattle on his 32,000-hectare (80,000 acre) ranch south of Cody, Wyoming, and on 16,000 hectares (40,000 acres) of Forest Service land on which he has grazing rights. For the first decade after he took over the ranch, he punched cows the conventional way. Since then, he's made some changes.

Turnell disagrees with the proposals by environmentalists to raise grazing fees and remove sheep and cattle from public rangeland. He believes that if ranchers are kicked off the public range, ranches like his will be sold to developers and chopped up into vacation sites, irreversibly destroying the range for wildlife and livestock alike.

At the same time, he believes that ranches can be operated in more ecologically sustainable ways. To demonstrate this, Turnell began systematically rotating his cows away from the riparian areas, gave up most uses of fertilizers and pesticides, and crossed his Hereford and Angus cows with a French breed that tends to congregate less around water. Most of his ranching decisions are made in consultation with range and wildlife scientists, and changes in range condition are carefully monitored with photographs.

The results have been impressive. Riparian areas on the ranch and Forest Service land are lined with willows and other plant life, providing lush habitat for an expanding population of wildlife, including pronghorn antelope, deer, moose, elk, bear, and mountain lions. And this *eco-rancher* now makes more money because the higher-quality grass puts more meat on his cattle. He frequently talks to other ranchers about sustainable range management; some of them probably think he has been chewing locoweed.

21. The fact that Turnell's decision-making process involves range and wildlife scientists is an example of   21.____

    A. successful government oversight
    B. enforced government regulation
    C. conventional ranching
    D. successful sustainable ranching

22. What is the environmental drawback to removing grazing animals from government range land?   22.____

    A. The loss of ranches which rely on public ranges to real-estate developers
    B. The loss of public range land to real-estate developers
    C. Under-use of public range land
    D. Increased vulnerability to forest fires due to under-use

23. Which of the following is a result of Turnell's decision to rotate his cattle?   23.____

    A. The production of cattle which tend to congregate less around water
    B. Increased bio-diversity which attracts and supports several animal species
    C. The production of beefier, more profitable cattle
    D. All of the above

24. Which of the following is an example of sustainable ranching?   24.____

    A. The use of pesticides to control disease
    B. Non-use of, and non-reliance on, public grazing lands
    C. Rotation of cattle away from riparian areas
    D. Independent decision-making

25. Which of the following is an effect of the increased diversity of plant life on the grazing land that Turnell uses?   25.____

    A. Production of leaner cattle
    B. Production of larger, meatier cattle
    C. Production of more abundant but less nutritious grasses
    D. Less reliance on pesticides

KEY (CORRECT ANSWERS)

1.	A		11.	B
2.	D		12.	C
3.	B		13.	A
4.	C		14.	A
5.	B		15.	D
6.	B		16.	B
7.	D		17.	D
8.	A		18.	A
9.	C		19.	C
10.	B		20.	B

21.	D
22.	A
23.	B
24.	C
25.	B

WORD MEANING
EXAMINATION SECTION
TEST 1

DIRECTIONS: For the following questions, select the word or group of words lettered A, B, C, D, or E that means MOST NEARLY the same as the word in capital letters. *PRINT THE LETTER OF THE CORRECT ANSWER IN THE SPACE AT THE RIGHT.*

1. The lane was NARROW and led to a mountain lake.   1._____

   A. attractive   B. not wide
   C. overgrown   D. rough
   E. without trees

2. Blow the horn as you APPROACH the gate.   2._____

   A. discover   B. leave
   C. draw near   D. pass through
   E. unlock

3. It was part of our BARGAIN that you should wash dishes.   3._____

   A. agreement   B. debt   C. goal   D. plan   E. wish

4. I shall remember that little valley FOREVER.   4._____

   A. often   B. yet   C. always   D. next   E. no more

5. The boy was EAGER to go on the trip.   5._____

   A. able   B. afraid   C. anxious   D. likely   E. willing

6. The children were having a DISPUTE over the boy.   6._____

   A. conversation   B. crying spell   C. disagreement
   D. performance   E. tantrum

7. The man was punished for his BRUTAL act.   7._____

   A. bloody   B. cruel
   C. deadly   D. defenseless
   E. ugly

8. We LAUNCHED our new business with great hope for the future.   8._____

   A. concluded   B. started   C. pursued   D. steered   E. watched

9. The two streets INTERSECT at the edge of town.   9._____

   A. run parallel   B. change names   C. end
   D. become thoroughfares   E. cross

10. She suffered from an UNCOMMON disease.   10._____

    A. ordinary   B. painful   C. contagious D. rare   E. new

11. The antique chair was very FRAGILE.   11.__

    A. delicate   B. worn   C. beautiful   D. well-made   E. useless

12. They picked EDIBLE mushrooms.   12.__

    A. poisonous   B. well-formed   C. unusual   D. large   E. eatable

13. He found the reception at the airport very GRATIFYING.   13.__

    A. surprising   B. deafening   C. pleasant
    D. disagreeable   E. impolite

14. DEFECTIVE brakes caused the mishap.   14.__

    A. old-fashioned   B. uneven   C. squeaking
    D. unused   E. faulty

15. After a little EXERTION the box was moved.   15.__

    A. argument   B. delay   C. coaxing   D. effort   E. planning

———

KEY (CORRECT ANSWERS)

1.	B		6.	C
2.	C		7.	B
3.	A		8.	B
4.	C		9.	E
5.	C		10.	D

11.	A
12.	E
13.	C
14.	E
15.	D

———

TEST 2

1. The RAPIDITY of the attack surprised us.   1._____

    A. power   B. effectiveness   C. possibility
    D. strangeness   E. swiftness

2. She enjoyed CONVERSING with her friends.   2._____

    A. meeting   B. laughing   C. talking   D. dining   E. traveling

3. There was a small VENT near the end of the tube.   3._____

    A. cap   B. screw   C. opening   D. joint   E. pump

4. With great CAUTION we opened the barn door.   4._____

    A. care   B. fear   C. distrust   D. danger   E. difficulty

5. The old man's coat was THREADBARE.   5._____

    A. spotted   B. tight   C. new   D. ill-made   E. shabby

6. I was sorry that I could not decide OTHERWISE.   6._____

    A. immediately   B. differently   C. favorably
    D. positively   E. eagerly

7. The GIGANTIC switchboard controlled all the lights in the theatre.   7._____

    A. complicated   B. up-to-date   C. automatic
    D. huge   E. stationary

8. The balls were made of SYNTHETIC rubber.   8._____

    A. artificial   B. hard   C. cheap   D. imported   E. crude

9. He was MERELY a servant in the house.   9._____

    A. occasionally   B. in no way   C. unhappily
    D. formerly   E. no more than

10. The prisoner CONFERRED with his lawyer.   10._____

    A. argued   B. interfered   C. dined
    D. sympathized   E. consulted

11. The soldier's GALLANTRY went unnoticed.   11._____

    A. strength   B. fright
    C. disobedience   D. injury
    E. bravery

12. The music was chosen for its SOOTHING effect.   12.___

    A. tuneful   B. calming   C. magic   D. exciting   E. solemn

13. The owners were advised to REINFORCE the wall.   13.___

    A. rebuild   B. lengthen   C. lower   D. strengthen   E. repaint

14. They performed their duties with UTMOST ease.   14.___

    A. noticeable   B. some   C. surprising   D. greatest   E. increasing

15. We picnicked near a CASCADE.   15.___

    A. pond   B. camp   C. waterfall   D. trail   E. slope

KEY (CORRECT ANSWERS)

1. E		6. B	
2. C		7. D	
3. C		8. A	
4. A		9. E	
5. E		10. E	

11. E
12. B
13. D
14. D
15. C

TEST 3

DIRECTIONS: For the following questions, select the word or group of words lettered A, B, C, D, or E that means MOST NEARLY the same as the word in capital letters. *PRINT THE LETTER OF THE CORRECT ANSWER IN THE SPACE AT THE RIGHT.*

1. The chairman was anxious to ADJOURN the meeting.   1._____

   A. conduct   B. attend   C. start   D. address   E. close

2. The gown was made of a GLOSSY fabric.   2._____

   A. shiny   B. embroidered   C. many-colored
   D. transparent   E. expensive

3. An ocean voyage in a small boat can be very HAZARDOUS.   3._____

   A. thrilling   B. slow   C. dangerous   D. rough   E. tiresome

4. The weatherman predicted VARIABLE winds.   4._____

   A. drying   B. strong   C. cool   D. light   E. changeable

5. Not long after the play began, the children began to FIDGET.   5._____

   A. clap   B. move restlessly
   C. cry   D. laugh aloud
   E. shriek

6. That person has a habit of MEDDLING.   6._____

   A. stumbling   B. interfering   C. play jokes
   D. cheating   E. being late

7. Young children are frequently INQUISITIVE.   7._____

   A. curious   B. saucy   C. restless   D. shy   E. tearful

8. The FALSITY of the report was apparent at first glance.   8._____

   A. uselessness   B. untidiness   C. incompleteness
   D. incorrectness E. disagreeableness

9. Orders were given to LIBERATE the prisoners by noon.   9._____

   A. question   B. transfer   C. free   D. sentence   E. fingerprint

10. She is HABITUALLY late for her dental appointments.   10._____

    A. usually   B. seldom   C. extremely   D. slightly   E. never

11. The soldiers were given SPACIOUS living quarters.   11._____

    A. pleasant   B. well-aired   C. crowded
    D. well-furnished E. roomy

12. The witnesses gave STRAIGHTFORWARD answers.   12.___

    A. hasty   B. frank   C. conflicting   D. helpful   E. serious

13. His income EXCEEDS that of his brother.   13.___

    A. is less regular than   B. is greater than
    C. is the same as   D. is less than
    E. is spent sooner than

14. He SHUNNED all of his neighbors.   14.___

    A. disapproved   B. welcomed   C. quarreled with
    D. avoided   E. insulted

15. Many of the natives are ILLITERATE.   15.___

    A. unable to read   B. unclean   C. unable to vote
    D. unmanageable   E. sickly

KEY (CORRECT ANSWERS)

1.	E		6.	B
2.	A		7.	A
3.	C		8.	D
4.	E		9.	C
5.	B		10.	A

11.	E
12.	B
13.	B
14.	D
15.	A

TEST 4

DIRECTIONS: For the following questions, select the word or group of words lettered A, B, C, D, or E that means MOST NEARLY the same as the word in capital letters. *PRINT THE LETTER OF THE CORRECT ANSWER IN THE SPACE AT THE RIGHT.*

1. We have always found this medicine to be RELIABLE. 1._____

   A. dependable   B. easy to use   C. pleasant-tasting
   D. bitter   E. fast-acting

2. The cloth was left to BLEACH in the sun. 2._____

   A. dry   B. soak   C. whiten   D. shrink   E. rot

3. The work is ORDINARILY done on time. 3._____

   A. seldom   B. without fail   C. necessarily
   D. hardly ever   E. usually

4. Jim is a very DISCOURTEOUS boy. 4._____

   A. impolite   B. daring   C. untruthful   D. uneasy   E. cautious

5. Paris is noted for its BOULEVARDS. 5._____

   A. crooked streets   B. parks   C. art galleries
   D. churches   E. broad avenues

6. The group formed the SEMICIRCLE quickly. 6._____

   A. half-circle   B. double circle   C. complete circle
   D. uneven   E. very small circle

7. The machine that he designed was PORTABLE. 7._____

   A. business-like   B. practical   C. of foreign manufacture
   D. easily transported E. difficult to use

8. The food supply DWINDLED during the winter. 8._____

   A. spoiled   B. became less   C. froze
   D. was wasted   E. was rationed

9. The vase was one of the PERMANENT exhibits at the museum. 9._____

   A. historical   B. lasting   C. popular
   D. artistic   E. well-planned

10. We could not understand why he left so ABRUPTLY. 10._____

    A. suddenly   B. soon   C. absent-mindedly
    D. mysteriously   E. noisily

KEY (CORRECT ANSWERS)

1.	A		6.	A
2.	C		7.	D
3.	E		8.	B
4.	A		9.	B
5.	E		10.	A

———

Basic Mathematics

EXAMINATION SECTION
TEST 1

DIRECTIONS: Each question or incomplete statement is followed by several suggested answers or completions. Select the one that BEST answers the question or completes the statement. *PRINT THE LETTER OF THE CORRECT ANSWER IN THE SPACE AT THE RIGHT.*

1. Add: 4,898 + 7 + 361 + 26   1.____

    A. 5,282   B. 5,292   C. 5,382   D. 5,392

2. Subtract: 7,006 - 5,797   2.____

    A. 1,209   B. 1,219   C. 1,309   D. 2,209

3. Multiply: $\begin{array}{r} 2,759 \\ \times\ 806 \\ \hline \end{array}$ 3.____

    A. 233,274   B. 2,173,754   C. 2,174,754   D. 2,223,754

4. Divide: $87\overline{)72,732}$ 4.____

    A. 835   B. 836   C. 846   D. 976

5. Combine: (+6)-(-4)+(-3)   5.____

    A. -1   B. +1   C. +7   D. +13

6. Simplify: [(-7)x(-8)] ÷ (-4)   6.____

    A. -14   B. -13   C. +13   D. +14

7. Add: 1 4/9 + 5 3/4   7.____

    A. 6 7/13   B. 6 7/36   C. 7 7/36   D. 7 12/36

8. Subtract: 5 4/7 - 3 3/4   8.____

    A. 1 23/28   B. 2 1/28   C. 2 1/3   D. 2 23/28

9. Multiply: 2 3/4 x 6 1/3   9.____

    A. 12 1/4   B. 13 1/4   C. 17 5/12   D. 18 5/12

10. Divide: 5 1/4 ÷ 1 1/2   10.____

    A. 3/7   B. 3 1/4   C. 3 1/2   D. 7 7/8

11. Add: 536.5 + .03 + 8.209   11.____

    A. .545009   B. .544739   C. 544.739   D. 545.009

12. Subtract: 879.3 - 57.64   12.____

    A. 3.029   B. 30.29   C. 821.66   D. 8216.6

13. Multiply: 4.87
    ×73.8

    A. 35.8406　　　B. 35.9406　　　C. 358.406　　　D. 359.406

13.__

14. Divide: $.053\sqrt{9.858}$

    A. 18.6　　　B. 18.7　　　C. 186　　　D. 187

14.__

15. Add: .5 + 1/4

    A. .075　　　B. .75　　　C. 5/4　　　D. 21/4

15.__

16. What is 4.4% of 48?

    A. 2.112　　　B. 10.90　　　C. 21.12　　　D. 211.2

16.__

17. 16 is what percent of 8?

    A. 1/2%　　　B. 5%　　　C. 50%　　　D. 200%

17.__

18. 24 is 48% of

    A. 2　　　B. 5　　　C. 50　　　D. 500

18.__

19. A set of stereo records sells for $26.00. It is discounted 12% for a special sale. What is the sale price?

    A. $3.12　　　B. $12.88　　　C. $14.00　　　D. $22.88

19.__

20.

Table A - Acme Mortgage Company
$320 Loan - 3/4 of 1% Interest

20.__

Month	Payment	Principal Paid/Month	Interest Paid/Month
1	$ 27.98	$ 25.58	$ 2.40
2	27.98	25.77	2.21
3	27.98	25.96	2.02
4	27.98	26.15	1.83
5	27.98	26.35	1.63
6	27.98	26.55	1.43
7	27.98	26.75	1.23
8	27.98	26.95	1.03
9	27.98	27.15	.83
10	27.98	27.35	.63
11	27.98	27.56	.42
12	27.93	27.77	.16
Total	$335.82	$320.00	$15.82

Acme Mortgage Company charges 3/4 of 1% (.0075) on the unpaid balance per month. Bowman Mortgage Company charges 8% per year on the total loan. Which company charges the MOST amount of interest on a $320 loan held for one year?

A. Bowman charges the most.　　B. Acme charges the most.
C. Acme and Bowman charge the same.　　D. Insufficient information to determine.

21.

21.____

Percent of Auto Insurance Discounts for High School Students with Certain Grade Point Averages

Policy Coverage	Grade Point Average Percent of Discount		
	A	B	C
Liability	33 1/3%	33 1/3%	10%
Comprehensive	20%	10%	-
Collision	25%	20%	-

Waldo Brown has an A average. The regular 6-month amounts to be paid for insurance before discounts follow:

Liability	$18.00
Comprehensive	$20.00
Collision	$60.00
Total	$98.00

How much does Waldo pay for insurance for 6 months?

A. $25.00   B. $48.00   C. $73.00   D. $146.00

22. Mrs. Ortiz had a fire in an apartment she owns. Repairing the damage will cost about $800. The apartment is valued at $11,000 and is insured for $10,000. Mrs. Ortiz had paid $28.00 a year for 12 years for her insurance. The insurance company will pay the full amount of the claim ($800).

22.____

Which of the following statements are TRUE?

  I.   The amount of the claim is more than the amount Mrs. Ortiz paid for the insurance.
  II. The insurance company should pay $11,000 for this claim.
  III. If the house had been completely burned, the insurance company would pay $11,000.
  IV. The maximum claim Mrs. Ortiz could collect is $10,000.

The CORRECT answer is:

A. I, IV   B. I, II   C. I, III   D. II, III

23. When two coins are tossed, what is the chance that both will be tails?
1 in _____.

23.____

A. 1   B. 2   C. 3   D. 4

24. If 5 teams are in a football league, how many games are necessary to allow each team to play every team one time?
_____ games.

24.____

A. 10   B. 15   C. 20   D. 25

25. Five women agreed to help collect money for the Salvation Army. They collected the following amounts: $43.00, $82.00, $16.00, $139.00, and $75.00.
What was the AVERAGE amount collected?

25.____

A. $70   B. $71   C. $75   D. $355

26. From the following statements, determine the CORRECT conclusion.
    I.   If Joe is a boxer, then Joe is strong.
    II. Joe is not strong.
    The CORRECT answer is:

    A. Joe is a boxer.
    B. Joe is not a boxer.
    C. Joe could be a boxer.
    D. All boxers are strong.

26.___

27. The graph represents the distribution of the Rexroth family budget. How much would the Rexroths have to earn per month if they are to save $1,800 per year?

    A. $150
    B. $1,650
    C. $1,800
    D. $21,600

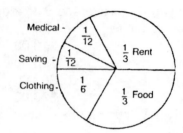

27.___

28.

	S	M	T	W	T	F	S
Mr. Tarver	?	8	8	8	8	8	3
Mr. Ramirez	1	8	9	9	8	8	5

Time and one-half is paid on Saturdays and for hours worked beyond 8 hours each day. Double-time is paid for Sunday work.
Mr. Tarver would have to work how many hours on Sunday to earn as much as Mr. Ramirez?

        Regular time - $2.00/hour
        Time and one - half - $3.00/hour
        Double time - $4.00/hour
        _____ hour(s).

    A. 1   B. 4   C. 5   D. 16

28.___

29. Dorothy Cook wrote the following four checks:
        $93.47 for a portable radio
        $113.57 for groceries
        $7.95 for gasoline
        $12.65 for utilities
    She deposited $42.96. The balance before the deposit and before the checks were written was $289.54. After the checks were written and the deposit made, what was her new balance?

    A. $61.90   B. $104.86   C. $227.64   D. $270.60

29.___

30. Given the formula I = PRT:
    If I = 27, R = .06, T = 3, find P.

    A.   .0067   B.   1.5   C.   4.86   D.   150.00

30.____

31. Fencing is needed to enclose a piece of
    land 24 meters on a side. How much
    fencing is needed? _____ meters.

    A.   48
    B.   96
    C.   384
    D.   576

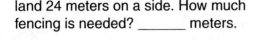
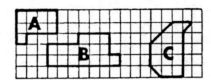

31.____

32. The area of figure A is 9 square units,
    and the area of B is 16 square units.
    What is the area of figure C? _____
    square units.

    A.   12
    B.   12 1/2
    C.   13
    D.   13 1/2

32.____

33. Using a 3 gallon spray can with a mixture rate of 1 teaspoon of insecticide per quart of
    water and an application rate of 1 gallon of mixture per 100 square feet, how much water
    and how much insecticide will be needed to spray a 75 feet by 10 feet lawn?
    _____ teaspoons of insecticide and _____ gallons of water.

    A.   30; 7 1/2   B.   30; 10   C.   15; 7 1/2   D.   20; 5

33.____

34. Frank Silva will carpet his living room
    which has the following dimensions.
    If Frank pays $6.00 per square yard for
    the carpet, how much will it cost to car-
    pet the living room? (9 square feet - 1
    square yard)

    A. $126
    B. $150
    C. $1,134
    D. $1,350

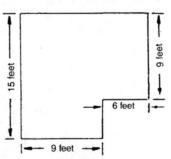

34.____

35. A cube is painted red and then divided
    into 27 smaller cubes. How many of the
    smaller cubes are painted on three sides
    only?

    A.   6
    B.   8
    C.   10
    D.   12

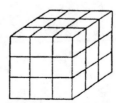

35.____

36. John and Frank wish to pour a cement walk 81 feet long, 4 feet wide, and 3 inches deep. If ready-mix concrete can be delivered on weekdays for $19.50 a cubic yard and on weekends for $22.50 a cubic yard, how much would be saved on the complete job if they decide to purchase the cement on Wednesday rather than on the weekend? (1 cubic yard = 27 cubic feet)   36.___

    A. $3.00   B. $9.00   C. $27.00   D. $58.50

37. Antifreeze may be purchased in different size containers for different prices.   37.___
        8 oz. can - 45¢
       10 oz. can - 53¢
       12 oz. can - 64¢
If exactly 15 pints of antifreeze are needed, how many cans of each size are needed for the cost to be minimum? (16 oz. = 1 pint)

    A. 10 - 12 oz. cans and 12 - 10 oz. cans
    B. 20 - 12 oz. cans
    C. 24 - 10 oz. cans
    D. 15 - 12 oz. cans and 6 - 10 oz. cans

38. From the graph, assuming the growth rate in the sophomore class is constant, how many students will be in the sophomore class in 2006?   38.___

    A. 325
    B. 350
    C. 375
    D. 400

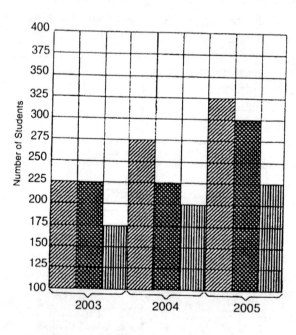

39.   39._____

Population in U.S.
1880 - 1980

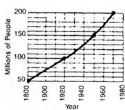

Percentage of the U.S.
Population in College

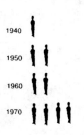

Key Each ▮ represents 1% of the population

In looking at the two graphs, which of the following conclusions are TRUE?
    I.   Both graphs cover exactly the same period of time.
    II.   Both graphs show population growth.
    III.   In 1950 there were 150 million people in the U.S. and 3 million college students.
    IV.   In the general population of 200 million in 1970, 8 million students were in college.
    V.   The percentage of the college students remains the same in the period 1940 to 1970.
    VI.   In 1920 there were only 1 million college students out of 100 million people.
The CORRECT answer is:

    A. I, II, III   B. II, III, VI
    C. II, V, VI   D. II, III, IV

40.   Martin Owens owns a mountain cabin that has a market value of $9,000. Its assessed   40._____
     value is 25% of the market value. The tax rate is $11 per $100 of assessed value.
     What is the amount of his tax?

    A. $24.75   B. $247.50   C. $495.00   D. $742.50

41.   To finance a new state highway system, you decide to raise the gasoline tax.   41._____
     What information would be MOST helpful in establishing the amount of the raise?
    I.   The total number of cars in the state
    II.   The total number of gallons of gasoline sold in the last year
    III.   The number of drivers under 21 years old
    IV.   A table showing a rate of increase in gasoline sold from year to year
    V.   A table showing the average number of miles driven per person
    VI.   The number of small (4 cylinder) cars in the state
    VII.   The number of car registrations sold each year
The CORRECT answer is:

    A. III, IV, VI   B. II, V, VII
    C. I, V   D. II, IV

42.

Income Tax Table

If adjusted gross income is		And the number of exemptions is -					
		1	2	3	4	5	6
At least	But less than	Your tax is -					
$2,450	$2,475	$236	$124	$23	$0	$0	$0
2.475	2.500	240	128	26	0	0	0
2.500	2.525	244	132	30	0	0	0
2.525	2.550	248	136	33	0	0	0
2.550	2.575	253	139	37	0	0	0
2.575	2.600	257	143	40	0	0	0
2.600	2.625	261	147	44	0	0	0
2.625	2.650	265	151	47	0	0	0
2.650	2.675	270	155	51	0	0	0
2.675	2.700	274	159	54	0	0	0
2.700	2.725	278	163	58	0	0	0
2.725	2.750	282	167	61	0	0	0
2.750	2.775	287	171	65	0	0	0
2.775	2.800	291	175	68	0	0	0
2.800	2.825	295	179	72	0	0	0
2.825	2.850	299	183	76	0	0	0
2.850	2.875	304	187	79	0	0	0

Alvie Ramos earned $2,856.00 during his senior year in high school. To find his adjusted gross income, he must reduce the amount earned by the standard 10% deduction. He had only one exemption, himself. How much tax did Alvie pay?

A. $139   B. $187   C. $253   D. $304

43.

Weight in Ounces	4 oz.	6 oz.	9 oz.	12 oz.	15 oz .
Price	2¢	4¢	7¢	10¢	13¢

Using the above table, predict the price if the weight in ounces is 25.

A. 23¢   B. 24¢   C. 26¢   D. 27¢

44. Given [(0,3),(1,5),(2,7),...(5,y)].
What is the value for y?

A. 9   B. 11   C. 13   D. 15

45. What is 4% of $14,000?

A. $560   B. $35   C. $56   D. $350

KEY (CORRECT ANSWERS)

1. B	11. C	21. C	31. B	41. B
2. A	12. C	22. A	32. C	42. C
3. D	13. D	23. D	33. A	43. A
4. B	14. C	24. A	34. A	44. C
5. C	15. B	25. B	35. B	45. A
6. A	16. A	26. B	36. B	
7. C	17. D	27. C	37. C	
8. A	18. C	28. B	38. C	
9. C	19. D	29. B	39. D	
10. C	20. A	30. D	40. B	

———

SOLUTIONS TO PROBLEMS

1. $4898 + 7 + 361 + 26 = 5292$

2. $7006 - 5797 = 1209$

3. $(2759)(806) = 2,223,754$

4. $72,732 \div 87 = 836$

5. $(+6) - (-4) + (-3) = 6 + 4 - 3 = +7$

6. $[(-7)(-8)] \div (-4) = \dfrac{56}{-4} = -14$

7. $1\ 4/9 + 5\ 3/4 = 1\ 16/36 + 5\ 27/36 = 6\ 43/36 = 7\ 7/36$

8. $5\ 4/7 - 3\ 3/4 = 5\ 16/28 - 3\ 21/28 = 4\ 44/28 - 3\ 21/28 = 1\ 23/28$

9. $(2\ 3/4)(6\ 1/3) = (11/4)(19/3) = 209/12 = 17\ 5/12$

10. $5\ 1/4 \div 1\ 1/2 = (21/8)(2/3) = 42/12 = 3\ 1/2$

11. $536.5 + .03 + 8.209 = 544.739$

12. $879.3 - 57.64 = 821.66$

13. $(4.87)(73.8) = 359.406$

14. $9.858 \div .053 = 186$

15. $.5 + 1/4 = .5 + .25 = .75$

16. $(4.4\%)(48) = (.044)(48) = 2.112$

17. $16/8 = 2 = 200\%$

18. $24 \div .48 = 50$

19. $\$26 - (\$26)(.12) = \$22.88$

20. Acme charges $15.82 in interest, whereas Bowman charges $(\$320)(.08) = \$25.60$ in interest. Thus, Bowman charges the most.

21. Total payment $= (\$18)(66\ 2/3\%) + (\$20)(80\%) + (\$60)(75\%) = \$73.00$

22. Statements I, IV are correct. Note that she paid $(\$28)(12) = \$336$ in insurance vs. the amount of the claim ($800). Also, since her house was insured for $10,000, that is the maximum amount she could receive for a claim.

23. Probability of 2 tails $= 1/2 \cdot 1/2 = 1/4 = 1$ in 4

24. $(5)(4) \div 2 = 10$ games. This is actually the number of combinations of 5 items taken 2 at a time.

25. ($43 + $82 + $16 + $139 + $75) ÷ 5 = $71

26. The conclusion is *Joe is not a boxer.* Let p = Joe is a boxer, q = Joe is strong. The contra-positive of *If p then q* is *If not q then not p.*

27. Earnings = (12)(savings), so that (12)($1800) = $21,600 earnings per year = $21,600 ÷ 12 = $1800 earnings per month.

28. Mr. Ramirez' earnings = (40)($2) + (7)($3) + (1)($4) = $105. So far, Mr. Tarver has earned ($40)(2) + ($3)(3) = $89.
    He needs to earn $16 on Sunday, which requires 4 hours.

29. New balance = $289.54 + $42.96 - $93.47 - $113.57 - $7.95 -$12.65 = $104.86

30. 27 = (P)(.06)(3), so P = 27 ÷ .18 = 150

31. Fencing needed = (24)(4) = 96 meters

32. Area of C = (4)(5) - (1/2)(2)(2) - (1/2)(1)(1) - 4 1/2 = 13 sq. units

33. (75)(10) ÷ 100 = 7.5 gallons of spray. Since 7.5 gallons = 30 quarts, 30 teaspoons of insecticide and 7 1/2 gallons of water are needed.

34. Area = (15)(15) - (6)(6) = 189 sq.ft. = 21 sq.yds.
    Then the cost = (21)($6) = $126

35. The cubes which are painted on 3 sides will be the 8 cubes in the corners.

36. Savings = [(27)(1 1/3)(1/12)] [$22.50 - $19.50] = $9.00

37. For A: Cost = (10)(.64) + (12)(.53) = $12.76
    For B: Cost = (20)(.64) = $12.80
    For C: Cost = (24)(.53) = $12.72
    For D: Cost = (15)(.64) + (6)(.53) = $12.78
    Option C has the minimum cost.

38. Growth rate = 50 per year. Number of sophomores in 2006 = 325 + 50 = 375

39. Statements II, III, IV are correct. Statement I is wrong since one graph covers 1880-1980, whereas the other graph covers 1940-1970. Statement V is wrong since the per-centage of college students increases from 1940 to 1970. Statement VI is unverifiable since the second chart does not include 1920.

40. Assessed value = (.25)($9000) = $2250. The tax = ($11)($2250/$100) = $247.50

41. The only statements pertinent to gasoline taxes would be II, V, and VII.

42. ($2856)(.90) = $2570.40. This number is found between $2550 and $2575 on the chart. Using the column for 1 exemption, the tax = $253.

43. The price in cents is 2 numbers below the number of ounces. Given 25 ounces, the price = 23 cents.

44. (5, y) corresponds to the sixth point. In the sequence 3, 5, 7,..., the sixth number is 13.

45. (.04)($14,000) = $560

———

ANSWER SHEET

TEST NO. _____ PART _____ TITLE OF POSITION _____

PLACE OF EXAMINATION _____ DATE_____

(CITY OR TOWN)   (STATE)

RATING

USE THE SPECIAL PENCIL.   MAKE GLOSSY BLACK MARKS.

Make only ONE mark for each answer.   Additional and stray marks may be counted as mistakes.   In making corrections, erase errors COMPLETELY.

ANSWER SHEET

TEST NO. ____________ PART ______ TITLE OF POSITION ________________________________
(AS GIVEN IN EXAMINATION ANNOUNCEMENT - INCLUDE OPTION, IF ANY)

PLACE OF EXAMINATION ________________________ (CITY OR TOWN) ________________ (STATE) DATE ________

RATING

USE THE SPECIAL PENCIL. MAKE GLOSSY BLACK MARKS.

1	A B C D E	26	A B C D E	51	A B C D E	76	A B C D E	101	A B C D E
2	A B C D E	27	A B C D E	52	A B C D E	77	A B C D E	102	A B C D E
3	A B C D E	28	A B C D E	53	A B C D E	78	A B C D E	103	A B C D E
4	A B C D E	29	A B C D E	54	A B C D E	79	A B C D E	104	A B C D E
5	A B C D E	30	A B C D E	55	A B C D E	80	A B C D E	105	A B C D E
6	A B C D E	31	A B C D E	56	A B C D E	81	A B C D E	106	A B C D E
7	A B C D E	32	A B C D E	57	A B C D E	82	A B C D E	107	A B C D E
8	A B C D E	33	A B C D E	58	A B C D E	83	A B C D E	108	A B C D E
9	A B C D E	34	A B C D E	59	A B C D E	84	A B C D E	109	A B C D E
10	A B C D E	35	A B C D E	60	A B C D E	85	A B C D E	110	A B C D E

Make only ONE mark for each answer. Additional and stray marks may be counted as mistakes. In making corrections, erase errors COMPLETELY.

11	A B C D E	36	A B C D E	61	A B C D E	86	A B C D E	111	A B C D E
12	A B C D E	37	A B C D E	62	A B C D E	87	A B C D E	112	A B C D E
13	A B C D E	38	A B C D E	63	A B C D E	88	A B C D E	113	A B C D E
14	A B C D E	39	A B C D E	64	A B C D E	89	A B C D E	114	A B C D E
15	A B C D E	40	A B C D E	65	A B C D E	90	A B C D E	115	A B C D E
16	A B C D E	41	A B C D E	66	A B C D E	91	A B C D E	116	A B C D E
17	A B C D E	42	A B C D E	67	A B C D E	92	A B C D E	117	A B C D E
18	A B C D E	43	A B C D E	68	A B C D E	93	A B C D E	118	A B C D E
19	A B C D E	44	A B C D E	69	A B C D E	94	A B C D E	119	A B C D E
20	A B C D E	45	A B C D E	70	A B C D E	95	A B C D E	120	A B C D E
21	A B C D E	46	A B C D E	71	A B C D E	96	A B C D E	121	A B C D E
22	A B C D E	47	A B C D E	72	A B C D E	97	A B C D E	122	A B C D E
23	A B C D E	48	A B C D E	73	A B C D E	98	A B C D E	123	A B C D E
24	A B C D E	49	A B C D E	74	A B C D E	99	A B C D E	124	A B C D E
25	A B C D E	50	A B C D E	75	A B C D E	100	A B C D E	125	A B C D E